D0563712

LEGACY OF
JOY

LEGACY OF
JOY

A Devotional for Fathers

Mike Nappa &
Dr. Norm Wakefield

PROMISE
PRESS
An Imprint of Barbour Publishing

Legacy of Joy—A Devotional for Fathers is another creative resource from the authors at Nappaland Communications, Inc. To contact the authors send e-mail to: Nappaland@aol.com

Unless otherwise noted, Scripture quotations are from the Holy Bible, New International Version (NIV), copyright © 1973, 1978, 1984 by the International Bible Society.

Published by Barbour Publishing, Inc., P.O. Box 719, Uhrichsville, Ohio 44683 http://www.barbourbooks.com

Member of the
Evangelical Christian
Publishers Association

Printed in the United States of America.

DEDICATION

For Tony.
You know what I liked best about today?
Being with you!
You're the reason I enjoy being a father.
Now, want to get whipped at
Quarterback Attack or Hall Hockey?

—*M. N.*

For all the men who have modeled a life of joy—
who have left to us a legacy.

—*N. W.*

CONTENTS

FOREWORD

As a child I never knew a dad's love. My father was no role model because he was the town alcoholic. Consequently, he didn't leave me a legacy of joy.

After I became a Christian, I reconciled with my dad. In fact, God allowed me to help him trust Christ for salvation. And in the last fourteen months of my father's life, he and I became close. Yet, that couldn't roll back the clock on a childhood void of a father's love. Without fatherhood modeled to me, I felt unprepared when I became a father myself.

You may not have had as poor of a relationship with your father as I did, but you undoubtedly share some realization that being a good dad in today's world isn't easy. We—and our children—live in a culture that is far from "family friendly." We live in a culture that has largely rejected biblical truth and moral absolutes. We live in a culture that threatens to capture our kids. Yet, we are faced with the challenge and awesome privilege to "train a child in the way he should go, and when he is old he will not turn from it" (Proverbs 22:6). But there is hope.

I admit to being a fellow struggler—a dad who desires to be a godly father, yet feels overwhelmed by the responsibility. That is why I avail myself of resources that equip me in practical fathering skills. And that's where Norm Wakefield, Mike Nappa, and this book come in.

I have known Norm for many years. He has become a role model to me. His profound insights into being a father after God's own heart have guided me through these many years. But more importantly, Norm doesn't just speak the truth; he *lives* the truth.

You will find *Legacy of Joy—A Devotional for Fathers* by Mike and Norm to be an invaluable resource for becoming a better dad. It can be a refreshing start to your busy day or a quiet moment at the end of your day.

Fathering is a God-given privilege—a grateful opportunity to impart our very lives to those we dearly love. And I thank God for men like Norm Wakefield and Mike Nappa who help us seize the moment and make every opportunity count for godly families.

JOSH MCDOWELL

THE CHOICE

Of all that was done in the past, you eat the fruit,
either rotten or ripe.
—T. S. Eliot

Choose for yourselves this day whom you will serve. . .But
as for me and my household, we will serve the Lord.
Joshua 24:15

He had a choice to make, that enterprising young man in Los Angeles. He wanted to visit his girlfriend. But how to get there? That was the question. Traffic was always a mess in L.A., which ruled out driving. After a few moments of thought, our hero made his choice. He would *fly* across town to where his girlfriend lived.

Not wanting to bother with an airplane, he took a lightweight lounge chair and attached several helium weather balloons to it. Grabbing a beer and an air pistol (to pop the balloons when he was ready to descend), this nameless Romeo settled into his chair and released it from the ground. He was flying! Comfortable with his drink, he chuckled at the poor suckers trapped in traffic on the freeway.

Then things began to go wrong. For starters, he accidentally dropped the air pistol and was unable to pop the weather balloons. His flying lounge chair kept ascending until it had reached 10,000 feet. The winds at that altitude blew him toward Los Angeles International Airport. A pilot flying nearby reported sighting a UFO. Should he have said he saw a man drinking beer in a lounge chair in air traffic lanes?

Avoiding collisions with stray airplanes, our hero leveled off at 15,000 feet. Fortunately, the helium was slowly leaking out of the balloons. Now he was gradually descending. A few hours after takeoff, the lounge chair came to rest in the backyard of a stranger's home—right by the swimming pool.

The choice this man made resulted in no real harm, but choices we make each day can have greater consequences. For example, remember

❖ The investor who figured a new soft drink
   named Coca-Cola must be a bad risk, so he
   sold his stock and invested in Raspberry Cola
   instead.

❖ The Scotsman who decided to push a piano up a mountain peak. It fell over a low cliff, dragging him behind it for 100 feet.

❖ The two Indonesian men who held a contest to see who could hold his breath the longest under water. They both drowned.[1]

❖ Or the father who chooses to give a legacy of pain instead of a legacy of joy to his children.

Heavenly Father, help us to recognize
the influence of today's choices
on the lives of our children tomorrow.

LEGACY OF PAIN

When the crime rate jumps, politicians promise to do
something about it. When the unemployment rate rises,
task forces assemble to address the problem. . . .
But when it comes to the mass defection of men
from family life, not much happens.
—David Blankenhorn (*Fatherless America*[2])

Weeping may remain for a night,
but rejoicing comes in the morning.
Psalm 30:5

Much as we hate to admit it, fathers today are known for leaving legacies of pain. Consider:

❖ Forty percent of U.S. children live in homes
   without a father present.
❖ Four out of five Americans rate the absence
   of a father from the home as "the most

significant social problem facing America."

❖ A majority of Americans believe that "most people have unresolved problems with their fathers."

❖ Today's teenagers report that they spend only about one hour each week in meaningful conversation with their fathers—less time than they spend watching television on an average day. Of teenagers living with a stepfather, a majority report that they spend no time at all in meaningful conversation with their stepdads.

❖ One out of four Americans say they cannot talk freely with their fathers.

❖ One of four American mothers report that the fathers of their children do not know what their children need to become mature and responsible.

Add to these statistics the all-too-common incidence of child abuse. Violence in the family is most likely perpetrated by men. Listen to these excerpts of actual childhood memories: "My grandfather molested me." "[I was] beaten, raped by my father." "My father used to burn me with a poker." "[I] was beat up by my father when he was drunk." "[I experienced] beatings by two stepfathers." "Father punched me through our storm door."

God never intended childhood memories to be like

these. As fathers, we can't choose whether to leave a legacy for our children—our children receive our legacy no matter what. But as fathers we can choose what kind of legacy we will leave—a legacy of pain, a legacy of absence, or a legacy of joy. Fathers have the power to impact the world from right within our families simply by choosing to leave the gift of joy in the childhood memories of our kids. It's these memories your kids will cherish the rest of their lives.

Fifteen years from now, your children will be answering the question, "What's one thing you remember about your father from your childhood days?" What would you like them to say?

Jesus, please use me to bring Your joy
that comes "in the morning."

DAD DIDN'T LEAVE ME
A LEGACY OF JOY

Your past is important, but it is not
important enough to control your future.
—Zig Ziglar (*Something to Smile About*[3])

For you know that it was not with perishable things
such as silver or gold that you were redeemed
from the empty way of life handed down to you
from your forefathers, but with the precious blood of
Christ, a lamb without blemish or defect.
1 Peter 1:18–19

"Mike and Norm, this idea of leaving a legacy of joy is well and good, but my father never gave me any such memories. I'm not sure I have something good to pass on to my own children."

Though you may not have a tradition to follow, you do have the power to start your own! You fathers who missed out on the legacy of joy from your own dads might actually have an edge on other fathers in one respect. You know the pain, so you have a stronger motivation to expend the energy needed to leave something better behind for your children.

Some adults who grew up in a positive home environment take joy and laughter for granted. They don't realize that it's something dads have to work at. But you know what you missed. Now you have the chance to make a new and greater commitment. The longing that may have attracted you to pick up this book is the drive you need to make you a winner.

We state this with a confidence that you probably do not feel yet. But it is a confidence that comes from personal experience. Neither of our dads knew how to impart joy to us. Sure, we've been tempted to complain about what we missed and to dwell on our own inadequacies. But God has taken the negatives in our childhood and turned them into positive desires to encourage joy-filled living in our families—and in yours. That driving desire has made us excited about the challenges of creating a legacy of joy.

It has happened—is still happening—for us. We don't want you to miss the fun.

Oh yes, it will feel awkward at first. But do you remember how you felt when you first learned to drive a car? Remember the goofy things you did, the mistakes you made? Now you settle behind the wheel and zoom off to your destination without giving the skills of turning the wheel and pushing the brake pedal a thought. You can also train your skills of communicating joy. You *can* have a joy-filled family environment.

Others have been this way before you. Even Jesus Christ desired to leave a legacy of joy for His "family." Listen to what He said to His disciples: "I have told you this so that my joy may be in you and that your joy may be complete" (John 15:11). You can be certain that God wants to empower you to pass on His joy to your children.

Your inner resolve to build a heritage of joy for your children will become something that will not only warm your children's hearts but will also leave you with a delightful sense of accomplishment. You just might have fun at it, too!

> *Lord Jesus, with Your help,*
> *I can move beyond my past*
> *and change my children's future.*
> *Give me courage to start today.*

CHECK YOUR "JOY QUOTIENT"

It is not selfish to be joyful.
—George MacDonald

So I commend the enjoyment of life,
because nothing is better for a man under the sun
than to eat and drink and be glad.
Ecclesiastes 8:15

No matter the circumstance, no matter your feelings, you can experience joy today—and share that joy with your children. To help you do that, we've created a little "Joy Quotient" quiz to help you assess your ability to spot the joys in everyday life. Take a moment right now to answer each question below with either a "true" or "false" and find your "joy quotient" rating.

1. Something made me smile today.
2. I have at least one hobby or activity I enjoy pursuing.

3. I have at least one good memory from my growing-up years.
4. I can see that God is present in my life (for example, by observing the beauty of creation, the faithfulness of a friend, or answers to prayer).
5. There is at least one thing I like about my work.
6. I sometimes dream of good things that could happen in my future.
7. I have at least one good memory from the past year.
8. I can think of at least one thing I like about each member of my family.
9. I feel proud about at least one thing I've accomplished in my lifetime.
10. I am confident that God loves me.

If you responded "true" as few as three times, you are probably feeling a bit burned out on life and wishing for more joy. Still, you have identified at least one reason to celebrate—so you can focus on that. Ask yourself how each positive response to these statements brings joy. How can you share that joy with your children? You also have an opportunity to include your kids as you search for new reasons to celebrate in life.

If you responded "true" four to seven times, you're about average. God didn't promise joy only to "above-average" people. You have plenty of reasons to celebrate and more reasons to include your children in the celebration.

If you responded "true" more than eight times, you've probably already begun sharing a bit of joy with those around you. One great thing about giving joy away is that you get joy in return. Read on to discover how we can do more of that.

Finally (though we hate to say it), if you answered "false" to all ten questions, you are lying to yourself and to us. Take a moment to ask God to show you joyful spots in your life. Then take the test again!

Father, give me eyes to recognize
the joy You've added to my life today.

LOOKING AHEAD

We grow great by dreams. All big men are dreamers.
They see things in the soft haze of a spring day
or in the red fire of a long winter's evening.
Some of us let these great dreams die,
but others nourish and protect them;
nurse them through bad days till they
bring them to the sunshine and light.
—Woodrow Wilson
(*Strength for a Man's Heart* [4])

There is surely a future hope for you,
and your hope will not be cut off.
Proverbs 23:18

Back in 1962, *Look* magazine asked the day's news-makers to dream a bit, envisioning the world as it would be near the end of the century.[5] Curious how they fared with their predictions? Judge for yourself. . .

❖ "In 25 years, either our lovely earth will be a charred lump of rubble circling the sun, or we shall all be well on our way to universal peace."—Irish playwright Sean O'Casey

❖ "I would expect the world to blush with shame to recall that, three decades earlier, a human being was graded by the color of his skin."—civil rights pioneer Martin Luther King, Jr.

❖ "One of the most exciting vehicles will be a family jet-powered sedan for five passengers. It will be capable of flying at speeds up to 500 mph."—Ben Kocivar, *Look* writer

❖ "The twenty-fifth anniversary of open tennis championships. . .will be held on Saturn."—Jack Kramer, general manager of Tennis Tournaments, Inc.

❖ "The Cold War will be a thing of the past. Internal pressure. . .for more freedom and the pressure of the masses for raising their living standards may lead to a gradual democratization of the Soviet Union."—David Ben-Gurion, prime minister of Israel

❖ "The 10-foot hoop will have been raised to 11.5 feet in '65, and another foot in '73."—University of California basketball coach Pete Newell

❖ "In the next 25 years, it is likely that man will create life in a test tube."—J. Robert Moskin, *Look* senior editor

❖ "Genocide. . .may be part of every country's foreign policy."—U.S. ambassador Clare Boothe Luce

❖ "Along with Lillian Russell and Mae West, [Marilyn Monroe] will live on as an enduring daydream figure of sex and wit."—Jack Hamilton, *Look* writer

❖ "A flyweight panel house, aluminum pipes to hold it up, a collapsible refrigerator, stove, and boat."—camping equipment predicted by industrial designers Raymond Loewy and William Snaith

❖ "A powerhouse Ivy League."—college football prediction by NFL commissioner Pete Rozelle

❖ "Parents will start bringing up their children, rather than vice versa."—historian Will Durant

❖ "Navel-baring [women's] fashions may help men bear the brave new world of 1987."—*Look* fashion editors

What do you dream for your children in the days ahead? What predictions would you make? Remember that the future grows out of the fertile soil of the present. If you want a rosy prediction for your children, make every effort to plant a few rosebush cuttings of joy in their lives today.

Creator God, please nourish the seeds
of joy we plant today,
so our children may have
a rose-colored future.

FOUR MEN,
FOUR STORIES

*What better feeling could a son have than
to know his father is pleased with him?*
—Cal Thomas[6]

*And a voice from heaven said, "This is my Son,
whom I love; with him I am well pleased."*
Matthew 3:17

Like it or not, you make a difference in the lives of your children. Your actions today leave an indelible mark. Consider Liam Gallagher.[7]

Liam is the lead singer for the British rock group Oasis. As a child Liam experienced physical and verbal abuse from his father. At twenty-four years of age, he recalled that his most vivid memory of his father was of watching helplessly as the man hit Liam's mother on the head with a hammer.

How did that image affect the child? "I stopped

believing in God because of what happened to me mam," he said in his thick British accent. Now Liam spreads a godless, fatherless message to millions through the music of his band.

Compare Liam Gallagher to Cal Thomas. Cal is a nationally syndicated columnist and a fervent, vocal Christian. Years after Cal's father died, he paused to reflect on the influence of his dad.

> What he did for a living was not the most important thing in my life, because it did not seem to be the most important thing in his. I do remember the Lionel train set he bought me one Christmas. I still have it and would not sell it at any price. I will never forget the hours he spent with me setting it up and watching the joy on my face as it raced around the track. I remember the backyard games of catch and the movies he took me to on Saturdays, back when movies were worth seeing. None of the things I remember about my father had anything at all to do with his lifestyle or whom he knew or the places he had been or the style of the clothes he wore. I just knew that he was always there.

Thomas carries a picture of his father in his briefcase, a constant reminder of the joy his father brought to childhood. In memory of his father, Liam Gallagher carries bitterness and resentment. "If he died tomorrow I wouldn't go to his funeral," says Liam.

In 1997 Lawrence Bridge unexpectedly died. He was only fifty-four. He was a missions pastor at a local church, a busy man with an important career. But when his family wrote his obituary for the local newspaper, they chose to remember him this way: "[Larry's] hobbies included Bible study, spending time with his children, and leading his family in a relationship with the Lord."

Three men. Three stories. Three memories.

Your story is the fourth. Make your actions today count.

Heavenly Father, help me recognize
the power of my actions today.

BATTLE SCARS
AND BLESSINGS

A careful man I must be,
Little children follow me.
I do not dare go astray,
For they will go the selfsame way.
—Anonymous

The memory of the just will be a blessing,
but the name of the wicked will rot.
Proverbs 10:7

"When I was a kid, my three older brothers and I used to fight like cats and dogs," states Norm. "We lived in the same house and carried the same family name, but we acted as though we were mortal enemies."

The persistent love of Jesus Christ corralled that unruly family. Those hostile relationships have been replaced with friendship and respect. Then Norm told of an incident that happened a couple of years ago on a stormy summer evening in western New York State:

"We were invited to the home of Ken's son, Rick, for supper. When we arrived, the smell of rain permeated the August air. One of those delightful summer thunderstorms broke loose with heaven's scenic fireworks. In the midst of barbecuing chicken and cooking corn on the cob, the electricity went out. So we ate our supper by candlelight.

"As often happens when an extended family gets together, our appetites were satisfied, and the 'Do you remember when. . . ?' began.

"Ken turned to Rick and said, 'I remember that night you and your brothers came into my bedroom after your mother and I had gone to sleep. You woke us up, and with tears running down your cheeks said, "I love you." God had spoken to your hearts in a powerful way during a youth group prayer time. As you verbalized your love for us, Joan and I were deeply moved.'

" 'The sweetness of those moments awakened thoughts about my dad,' Ken continued. 'I realized that I had never told him that I loved him. I'd expressed lots of anger and resentment when I was a teenager, but never gratitude or love. So the next day I penned a letter to him expressing appreciation for what he had invested in my life and asked forgiveness for the grief I'd caused him. In a week or so a letter arrived from Dad. It was the only letter he ever wrote to any family member that I knew of. He told how much he loved us children and how proud he was of each one. It was probably the most precious letter I ever received.'

"By now tears were streaming down Ken's cheeks. His son Rick also was weeping. Ken's grandson, Ricky, Jr., was leaning against his granddad's shoulder, watching father and grandfather share a tender, sacred memory. He too was feeling the moment.

"I was struck with the significance of this evening. I could see Ricky, Jr., relating this incident to his children and later to his grandchildren. I could see those children listening with joy as a heritage of love was passed on."

Wouldn't it be great if your children, grandchildren, and great-grandchildren could experience a moment like that?

Dear Lord, help me capture the moments
and share them with my children today.

FREEZE-FRAME MEMORIES

I want my children to remember:
Mom and Dad love each other.
Home is a happy place to be.
—H. B. London, Jr.
(*The Minister's Little Devotional Book*[8])

A happy heart makes the face cheerful,
but heartache crushes the spirit.
Proverbs 15:13

"He was laughing so hard that tears streamed down his face like little rivers of joy that stained his cheeks," says Mike. "It was hard to believe he had buried his mother a few hours earlier. But that was my grandfather, a man we called 'Jidee,' and a man who chose to mix a little joy into the drink we called grief.

"They had been close, Jidee and great-grandmother. He had cared for her for many years, faithfully stopping by her home each day to see that she was warm and fed. He planned each day around seeing his mother. She lived a long, full life.

"When the day came for her to leave this earth, my grandfather called me at college. 'Please come home for the funeral,' he said. 'I'll pay for your plane ticket.' I came, and my sisters and I all cried tears of sorrow during the service.

"Later, exhausted, we retreated to Jidee's house. As we sat in somber silence, a smile flickered on my grandfather's face. He was remembering those special times a mother shares with her son. Curious, we begged him to tell us about growing up as an immigrant in the early 1900s.

"For the next two hours he regaled us with stories of his mother, his brother, his aunts and uncles. We laughed and cried and shouted and sighed and mourned and rejoiced all at the same time. And it was then he passed a bit of his legacy on to me, his grandson. A legacy that reminds me that there is joy to be found today, even in the midst of sorrow."

Norm tells a different kind of joy story about the day he decided to surprise his nine-year-old daughter, Jody:

"She had a passion for horses and *The Black Stallion* was playing at our local theater. I drove to Lookout Mountain Elementary School. I explained to the secretary that I was Jody's dad and needed to take her out of school for the afternoon. We had an important event to attend. I hurried to her classroom and announced to the teacher that Jody was excused for the rest of the day.

"When we got outside, she looked at me curiously and said, 'How come you're taking me out of class?'

"I replied, 'You remember that movie you said you can't wait to see? Let's go see it now!'

"Her eyes lit up with delight. A big grin spread from ear to ear. She was absolutely thrilled that I had interrupted her day with the fun news. Years later she told me how much that surprise afternoon had meant to her—I had 'wowed' her! And I'm mighty glad that I acted on my impulse to share an afternoon of joy with Jody."

Holy Spirit, prompt my heart today
to spontaneously spread
Your joy to my family.

MAKING MEMORIES

*No soul that seriously and constantly
desires joy will ever miss it.*
—C. S. Lewis (*The Great Divorce*)

*Be joyful in hope,
patient in affliction,
faithful in prayer.*
Romans 12:12

What's one thing you remember about your father from your childhood days? We asked several people at random. Here's what they had to say:

❖ "We went walking on a Sunday afternoon. It
    was really pretty, and I was so tired that he put
    me on his shoulders. I covered his eyes, so we
    kept on bumping into things! But it was just
    the two of us, taking time out together. I'll

always remember that."—twenty-year-old woman from England

❖"One thing I remember about my dad was that he was always working. I hardly got to see him when I was younger because he was always working. I guess it paid off. We have a lot of stuff."—twenty-one-year-old man from California

❖"He always pushed me in my sports."—nineteen-year-old woman from Michigan

❖"I remember we'd go to amusement parks and I was too short for the rides, but he wanted me to be able to enjoy the ride. He'd pick up my shoulders and pull up my hair and do whatever he could to get it above the line. That's what I remember about my dad."—twenty-three-year-old man from Arizona

❖"The very first thing I remember about my dad is that he wasn't there a lot. My parents weren't divorced or anything, but he was a fireman and had to work a number of jobs to support our family. I think he missed us."—twenty-year-old woman from Colorado

❖"I remember sneaking out of our bedroom with my brothers and sisters. We could see Daddy watching TV, but he was always very focused on TV so he'd never see us."—twenty-four-year-old woman from California

❖ "We'd always wrestle around on the couch after dinner. Me and my brothers always goof off and wrestle around. We'd all end up laughing! We were laughing a lot. I remember my dad was a happy guy."—eighteen-year-old man from California

Memories like these become the foundation for the legacy your children inherit from you, and the impression points by which your children form their view of God, our heavenly Father. If your children remember that you were never available to them, your legacy is abandonment (whether you live with your kids or not). If your children remember you as someone who constantly criticized, your legacy will be dissatisfaction.

Imagine how your daughter's life will be different if, instead of remembering a frown on dad's face, she sees your smile. Think what changes might occur if your son remembers, not the hours you put in at the office, but the hours you spent playing with him.

By creating happy memories for your children, you create a legacy of joy to pass on from generation to

generation. That's exactly what your heavenly Father—
and your children—want.

Heavenly Father, use me to create
a happy memory for my children today.

SMART DADS I KNOW

A father's heart brings love. . .his arms, comfort. . .
his words, trust. . .his example, instruction. . .
his smile, confidence. . .his presence, joy!
—Author unknown

He who fears the Lord has a secure fortress,
and for his children it will be a refuge.
Proverbs 14:26

In 1975 Charlie Shedd wrote an excellent book called *Smart Dads I Know.*[9] He describes men who used creativity and perseverance to overcome obstacles and build strong father/child relationships. The book challenged us to be deliberate and thoughtful in making parenting both fun and fruitful.

Charlie told about Bob, a long-distance truck driver. His job required him to travel ten days at a time, from Kenosha, Wisconsin, to the West Coast. This dad was determined not to let his long absences undermine his family life. His wife described Bob this way:

"Bob's the very best. When he is home, you should see the way the kids spend all their time with him. Drop everything to be there. They think he's the greatest."

Bob knew how to turn a liability into an asset. He'd often take one of his children on his long-distance run, just the two of them together. What child wouldn't like to ride in the cab of a big semi? Because Bob was imaginative, he made it a big adventure.

Emmett, too, worked long hours during the week and had to travel. But he guarded his weekends for his family. In addition to family activities, Emmett reserved at least one hour for each child each weekend—just for the two of them. What did they do?

"Sometimes I just sit in their bedroom and we visit. We might go out to breakfast. Or shop for something they need. Play catch. Watch one of their favorite TV shows. But you can bet each one gets sixty minutes."

Most dads have some adversity to overcome in parenting. We liked the love and creativity one dad exhibited. He was a single-parent dad raising his daughter alone. Here is the daughter's account after she was an adult.

"When I started school, my father gave me ten cents. He said, 'Patty, I want you always to keep this dime in your purse. Anytime you need me, you call me at the plant. Tell them you want to talk to your dad, and I guarantee they'll let you right through.'

"There is no way I could tell you what that ten cent piece from my father meant. Even when I didn't need him, just to know I had it in my purse made me feel secure."

What is the adversity that keeps you from being the "smart dad" you want to be? One friend has gone through a painful divorce. His devotion to his four children is evident, and he has learned how to turn exhausting problems into opportunities. In spite of his divorce, we're certain that his children will rise up and call him "blessed." With a little creativity and perseverance you, too, can plant joy in the lives of your children. When that happens, you, like Patty's dad, give your child something special to write about later.

Jesus, please make me a "smart dad."

THIRD-GENERATION
DECISIONS

*The man who has not learned to say No will be
a weak if not wretched man as long as he lives.*
—Alexander Maclaren

*These commandments that I give you today are to be upon
your hearts. Impress them on your children. Talk about
them when you sit at home and when you walk along the
road, when you lie down and when you get up.*
Deuteronomy 6:6–7

One mark of great men is the decisions they make about
such vital issues as their children.

Take Eddie Basha, for example. His family had built
a respected grocery chain in Arizona. He was active in the
political scene, a candidate for governor. But Eddie
dropped out of the governor's race and left political life.

"I want time to go to soccer games with my sons. I

want time for tennis lessons with my sons. I want to be able to be here at night for them. I don't want to be at some meeting speaking. I want to grow up with them. They're eight and ten, and they need a father.

"My dad died when he was fifty-seven. And I said, 'You know, every day after my dad's fifty-seventh birthday is kind of a gift.' And I want to give those days that I have to my children."

Or, consider James Dobson. Twenty years ago he was rising fast as a spokesman for the family. His calendar was full from speaking engagements, writing, and teaching responsibilities. Dobson, like Basha, faced that crucial question, "What's most important?"

Dobson's decision was prompted by his own father's death. He reminisced on the profound influence his dad had on his life and times they had hiked together in the woods. Now at his dying father's bedside he asked himself, "What will my kids recall when I'm dying?" So Dobson curtailed his speaking engagements for a time to schedule more time with his children.

Matt Williams's decision cost him $2.5 million. Williams was a premier third baseman in the major leagues, some would say the best. In 1997 he hit thirty-two homers, drove in 105 runs, and won his fourth Gold Glove. But Matt played baseball in Cleveland, Ohio, and his children lived in Scottsdale, Arizona, separated by divorce.

Matt's dad had left a heritage of joy. He was not only an excellent carpenter but a great dad. Mom and dad invested in his life and were there for him every day. He wanted to pass that heritage on to his own children.

So when Williams had the opportunity to be traded to an expansion team, the Arizona Diamondbacks, he jumped at the chance, even though it cost him a $2.5 million pay cut. "My children are my life. Being with them is what it's all about."

These men teach us an important lesson: Children find joy in the simple presence of fathers. An absent father's presents can never make up for being present in a child's life.

Did you notice that each of these decisions was influenced by the example of a father? It makes a person wonder what our example will mean to our children's life decisions.

Dear God, give me wisdom
to make decisions that allow me to
be an example of a joyfully committed father.

WHICH WAY ARE YOU GOING?

A six-year-old girl is a joy to be around.
—William Burks, Jr.[10]

Thus you will walk in the ways of good men
and keep to the paths of the righteous.
Proverbs 2:20

I n 1856 in a cemetery outside Chicago, Illinois, someone
left the following tombstone inscription:

> Remember, man, as you pass by,
> As you are now, so once was I.
> As I am now, so you shall be,
> So prepare yourself to follow me.

At some later date a creative person taped two additional
lines to the inscription:

To follow you is not my intent,
Until I know which way you went![11]

Some individuals follow others without thinking whether their way is really what is best. They may be attracted to a winsome personality, a skill, or fame, but they don't consider the consequences of that person's lifestyle, values, or relationships.

William Burks, Jr., didn't want to do that. William Burks, Sr., was a hard-working man of moral conviction. He impressed on young William the importance of honesty. But William, Sr., also worked long, exhausting hours to provide for his family. By the time he was fifteen years old, William, Jr., says, "I made a vow that when I had children, they were going to know me. Good or bad, they would know me."

He finished college, got married, and started his career with the best of intentions. But he had inherited a workaholic's legacy. He soon discovered that the Burks' habit of being consumed with work had attached itself to him. As children were born, the same career demands that had kept William, Sr., from being with his children were now at work in William, Jr. He buried himself in long hours and a successful career.

Finally his wife said to him, "William, what we need around here is a father and a husband. We don't need a slave. That's what you've become to those businesses."

The indictment stung with the truth. William recognized circumstances that indicated the Lord was redirecting his steps. He began to refocus his life so he could devote more time to his family. And he discovered that God made full provision for the family.

Now he wanted to protect his son from making his mistakes. So he sat the boy down to talk about his childhood, how he felt robbed of the joy of having his father around and how he had been guilty of doing the same thing.

As the father-son chat began to wind down, William, Jr., remarked, "Well, Son, I'm telling you all this because I can see you falling into the old Burks' habits. I know how hard it is to leave that desk when it's piled so high. But your little girl is never going to be six years old again. Your being with her is a gift beyond price and will forge a bond stronger than any iron your farrier granddad ever hammered."

Time will tell whether William, Jr., helped his son overcome a negative inheritance. For now we must ask: Have we learned the lesson William, Jr., sought to pass on to his son?

Father, teach us to grasp opportunities to enjoy our children, to see them as Your gift to us.

THE LAUGHTER FACTOR

There is hardly a system in the body
a hearty laugh doesn't stimulate.
—William F. Fry, M.D. (*1001 Humorous Illustrations*[12])

A cheerful heart is good medicine.
Proverbs 17:22

There's a reason why the child who can barely drag himself out of bed in time for school during the week is up at the crack of dawn to watch cartoons on Saturdays. Cartoons make him laugh.

William F. Fry of Stanford University has studied the medical effects of humor since 1953. He has proven that King Solomon was right: A cheerful heart is good medicine. Something as simple as laughing makes us feel better all over, partly because laughter stimulates the production of hormones that release endorphins in the brain. Those endorphins give us a sense of pleasure and contentment.

Stanley Tan and Lee Berk of the Loma Linda University School of Medicine find that people who laugh are less likely to suffer from colds and flu because laughter stimulates the immune system. This link between joviality and health is so well established that many doctors use "humor therapy" as part of a comprehensive cancer treatment program. Humor is good activity for the healthy as well. Consider:

- ❖ Laughing is a tension-buster. A good chuckle reduces stress and aids relaxation.
- ❖ One hundred laughs gives the same amount of aerobic exercise as ten minutes on a rowing machine.
- ❖ Laughing involuntarily exercises your abdomen as well as fifteen facial muscles.

Dr. Fry's research has revealed that:

- ❖ A healthy guffaw stimulates lungs, circulation, and muscle tone.
- ❖ Protracted chuckling "massages right down to the toes and fingertips."
- ❖ Laughter works out the shoulders, back, and diaphragm.

According to tests done by Swedish psychologist, Lars Ljungdahl, laughter is good for mental health as well:

- ❖ Laughter is effective at combating depression.
- ❖ Laughter creates a heightened sense of mental well-being.
- ❖ Laughter helps the mind to think creatively.[13]

Unfortunately, we men have forgotten how to laugh. If you're an average American man, researchers say you laugh fifteen times a day. Your children, however, will laugh, chuckle, giggle, snicker, and guffaw more around 400 times before they nod off to sleep tonight! Your wife is 127 times more likely to laugh than you are.

Laughter is contagious. When you laugh with your family, you spread "joy germs" to your kids and plant seeds of laughter. And they gain one more happy memory of time spent with you. Once you become a laughing father, you're well on your way to leaving a legacy of joy for your kids.

Holy Spirit, help me make laughter
the light that warms my home.

LASTING LAUGHTER

God picked my dad out just for me because
God has a very good sense of humor.
—Anonymous child
(*Kids Say the Cutest Things About Dads*[14])

I have told you this so that my joy may be
in you and that your joy may be complete.
John 15:11

What will be the last memory your family members have of you?

Judy Price's last memory of her dad, Bob Armstrong, was hearing his hearty laughter as he played with his grand-daughter. When Judy looked in on them, she found grand-father and granddaughter on the floor romping. He was wearing a ring in his nose and earrings in his ears. The two of them were laughing, acting silly, and having tons of fun.

Bob was a pilot for Scenic Air Lines. He died a few

days later when his aircraft crashed near Montrose, Colorado. In a moment, he was gone, and Judy and her daughter were left with powerful, positive memories. The memories filled hearts with warmth and laughter long after Bob's last day on earth. "He was just one of those people that, if you came in contact with him, you loved him. Fun is really the only word I can use to describe him. He was such a wonderful father."

We've heard lots of people relate their memories of fathers and grandfathers. Many memories are not happy:

- ❖ "He was a good man but he never seemed to have time for me. He was more interested in his dirt bikes than in his daughters."
- ❖ "I've been scared of my dad all my life. He used threats to control me, and I knew they were real."
- ❖ "My grandfather abused me when I was five years old. I still don't know how to get free of the bitterness."
- ❖ "Dad and mom divorced when I was three. Dad came around a few times but then seemed to drift away and never returned."

Three thousand years ago a wise man wrote, "The memory of the righteous will be a blessing, but the name of the wicked will rot" (Proverbs 10:7). Every day we are given a new opportunity to make deposits in someone's memory bank. Bob Armstrong invested a few minutes of laughter, and that investment continues to refresh, delight, and energize. Positive memories will give joy and hope to those we love. What better investment could we make?

Lord God, help me share the humor
You've placed in my heart.

LAUGHING PLACES

*My brother (Roy) called me in and said that we owed
the bank four-and-one-half million dollars. And I
begin to laugh. And he said, "What are you laughing at?"
And I said, "I was just thinking back when we couldn't
borrow a thousand dollars."*
—Walt Disney

*He will yet fill your mouth with laughter
and your lips with shouts of joy.*
Job 8:21

What makes you laugh? A funny joke? A comedic
movie? A late-night talk show host? As Bre'r Rabbit
so eloquently put it in the classic Walt Disney movie, *Song
of the South,* "Ev'rybody has a laughing place. Hahaha!"
You just have to look for it.

When journalist Norman Cousins was diagnosed
with a degenerative spinal tissue disease, doctors gave him

a one-in-five-hundred chance of recovery. He had every reason not to laugh, but he instead devised his own daily "humor prescription."

Norman went out of his way to spark laughter each day. He watched reruns of the old television show, *Candid Camera,* took in old Marx Brothers movies, and partook of all the humor he could find. And he made a remarkable recovery, due in part to his determination to find a reason to laugh each day.

Richard Lederer isn't suffering a debilitating illness, but he finds a laughing place in the unintentional blunders we make with this complex language called English. Here are a few chuckle-makers from his book, *More Anguished English:*[15]

- ❖ From music class papers: "Most authorities agree that music of antiquity was written a long time ago." . . . "Do you know that if Beethoven were alive today, he'd be celebrating the 160th anniversary of his death?"
- ❖ From church bulletins: "Tomorrow's lecture will be 'Recycling—Our Garbage is a Resource.' There will be a potluck supper at 6 p.m." . . . "The peace-making meeting scheduled for today has been canceled due to a conflict."
- ❖ From newspaper headlines: "New Study of

Obesity Looks for Larger Test Group." . . .
"Here's How You Can Lick Doberman's Leg
Sores.". . . "Cops Quiz Victim in Fatal
Shooting."

❖ From advertisements: "Try our cough syrup.
You will never get any better." . . . "An unex-
pected vacancy for a knife-thrower's assistant.
Rehearsals start immediately."

Robert Wayne Pelton finds his laughing place in
"loony laws" he's discovered:[16] In Ottumwa, Iowa, it's illegal
for a man to wink at a woman he doesn't know. . . . In Texas,
when two trains meet at a crossing, it's illegal for either train
to proceed until the other has passed. . . . In Winchester,
Massachusetts, "A young lady cannot be employed to dance
on a tightrope, except in church." . . . Salem, West Virginia,
law prohibits the eating of candy during the hour and a half
before attending a church meeting. . . . In Memphis,
Tennessee, it's illegal for frogs to croak after 11 p.m.

Laughable moments are sprinkled everywhere. It's
up to you to find—and laugh at—them.

Dear God, give me eyes to spot the laughing places
in my life and in the lives of my children.

EMPEROR NORTON

My deeds will be measured not by my youthful appearance, but by the concern lines on my forehead and the laugh lines around my mouth.
—Erma Bombeck, from her last column before dying of cancer

Blessed are you who weep now, for you will laugh.
Luke 6:21

Some called him crazy. Others called him a fool. But most San Franciscans in the late 1800s called him Emperor.

Emperor Norton, that is.

His official title was "Emperor of the United States and Protector of Mexico." He "ruled" San Francisco from 1857 to 1880, spreading smiles and joviality. He was just a man with a happy attitude, a merchant who had tried to corner the rice market—and lost his fortune. Yet, after going from riches to poverty, Norton refused to accept that he had to lose his joy. He "crowned" himself and began parading around the streets of San Francisco in full costume as emperor.

There was something so appealing about a man who insisted on enjoying life that the people of the city by the bay went along with the charade. The good king was granted front row seats at every theatre opening. Tailors carefully created and mended his regal plumed hat, cane, and uniform at no cost. The finest restaurants served this monarch their best meals free. The railroads offered transportation "so he could address his subjects." Emperor Norton even had an honorary seat in the state legislature!

How did a man with few financial means earn such a lavish lifestyle? He dealt in a currency that's all too rare—the currency of smiles. His majesty always brought a smile to the faces of others; like the time he ordered a bridge be built to span the bay—the Golden Gate Bridge; or when he decreed that a giant Christmas tree be raised in Union Square for the children of his kingdom.

We fathers can learn a lot from this would-be sovereign. If we would win the hearts of our children, we must be willing to share with them a simple, lasting joy that Jesus gives to life. When we do, our children, like the people of San Francisco, will remember us with fondness.

Funny thing about Emperor Norton. You, too, have

probably gotten a little joy from this so-called crazy man. Mark Twain immortalized the emperor in the character of his pauper "king" in the classic novel *The Adventures of Huckleberry Finn*. If you've read the book, you, too, have met the emperor of the United States and protector of Mexico.

Dear Jesus, teach me to enjoy life
like a man who rules the world!

EXPERIMENTING IN SMILES

Smile—It's the second-best thing your lips can do.
—bumper sticker

But may the righteous be glad and rejoice before God;
may they be happy and joyful.
Psalm 68:3

On a trip to Japan, Siu Wa Tang, chairman of the Department of Psychiatry at the University of California, Irvine, couldn't understand why his hosts obviously disliked his associate. The companion had done nothing to offend, but he was treated frostily. Tang decided the Japanese must not like the look on the associate's face. He tested his theory.

Tang made photographic slides of faces expressing anger, contempt, disgust, fear, happiness, sadness, and surprise. Nine of ten Americans accurately identified the emotion intended by each expression. But Tang was amazed by the miscommunication of the faces in Japan. Most Americans quickly identified the man in one picture as expressing fear, but most Japanese thought the man pictured was sad or mildly surprised.

There was at least one exception to this facial confusion, however. Among Americans or Japanese, a smiling face was always identified with "happiness." A smile could be a universal language.

Mike found that out when he hurriedly stopped by the grocery store one evening. He made his purchase and walked briskly out the door. A few paces ahead was a woman, heading in the same direction.

"Since I was moving at a faster pace, I quickly began to catch up to her. She shot a quick glance my way. I must have been frowning, or at least had a serious expression, because as soon as she saw me closing the gap between us, her eyes flew open in alarm. She interpreted my actions as threatening.

"I deliberately slowed and walked a wide circle around her to get to my car. But that moment caused me to think about the messages my face sends out. I determined to try to smile in public. Now, when I pass a stranger, I smile and nod. When I'm driving down the street and notice the driver next to me glancing my way, I flash a grin. Sometimes I feel like I'm forcing my lips to curl upward, but the response has been rewarding.

"Sour-faced drivers look surprised, then invariably return the smile (and let me switch lanes later when my lane suddenly ends). Folks at Wal-Mart do a double-take, then smile back and pause to hold the door open for my wife. Surly teenagers in black leather and ripped jeans relax and grin greetings my way.

"Occasionally some sourpuss will frown and mutter, but at least I'm no longer frightening poor women in parking lots. And I've learned to take that smile home. I find my family willing to give plenty more in return."

Are you the frowning dad? The mourning dad? The scary dad? The worried dad? Or the smiling dad? Get in the habit of sharing a smile or two with your children today!

Heavenly Father, help me remember that
knowing You is reason enough to smile.

TICKLISH MOMENTS

Laughter is the brush that sweeps
away the cobwebs of the heart.
—Mort Walker

Our mouths were filled with laughter,
our tongues with songs of joy.
Psalm 126:2

Shrieking laughter, squirms, giggles, wiggles. After ten seemingly endless seconds, Mike's seven-year-old son, Tony, finally sat smiling and gasping for breath on the family room floor.

Mike and Tony had bet a ten-second tickle-fest on whether Mike could make an indoor basketball shot. Mike won the bet, so Tony had to endure the tickling. Mike thought he might run away, but Tony braced and smiled for the "attack." With Mom counting, the tickle-fest commenced. Of course, Tony's mom lost count a couple of times, dragged out the numbers, and generally delayed getting to ten for as long as possible. Finally the torture was over, and Mike relented.

As he lay wheezing on the floor, Tony turned to his mother and said with emphasis, "That was probably the best ten seconds of my entire life!"

That ten seconds of precious memory didn't cost a dime. It didn't take an expensive electrical toy, or a trip to an amusement park, or even a new stuffed animal. All it cost was Mike's willingness to tickle or be tickled.

Says Mike, "That's what I want to give my son—a lifetime filled with laughter and a legacy of joy." Still, it's easy to forget the importance of passing that kind of heritage on to our children. Instead of planting laughter, we inadvertently plant sorrow.

Philip Yancey, in his wonderful book, *What's So Amazing About Grace,*[17] tells a brief story of a friend of his named George who did just that. George's marriage had gone through angry, difficult times. Finally one night, George reached his breaking point, pounded the table and the floor, and screamed, "I hate you!" at his wife. "I won't take it anymore! I've had enough! I won't go on! I won't let it happen! No! No! No!"

The couple managed to stay together, working to repair the broken relationship. Then, months later, George was awakened by noises from the bedroom of their two-year-old son. George listened at his son's door, and shivers ran through his flesh. In a soft voice, the two-year-old was repeating word for word with precise inflection, "I hate you! . . . I won't take it anymore! . . . No! No! No!"

Yancey writes, "George realized that in some awful way he had just bequeathed his pain and anger and unforgiveness to the next generation."

Your child only gets one childhood. You can fill it with shrieks of laughter and tickles or cries of anger and pain. Which will you choose?

Holy Father, remind me again how fun it is to laugh,
and how much more fun it is to see
my child laughing as well.

WHAT'S A KID WORTH?

Children are our most valuable natural resource.
—Herbert Hoover

But God demonstrates his own love for us in this:
While we were still sinners, Christ died for us.
Romans 5:8

What's a child worth?

Sadly some place no value on children. During one two-week period recently, four newborn infants were "discarded" as worthless. One baby was found in a trash dumpster. Another was left in the toilet of a ladies' restroom at an amusement park. The third was placed in a cardboard box and abandoned in front of a day care center. The fourth was killed by its mother.

Men and women who follow Jesus Christ are guided by the principle in Psalm 127:3: "Sons are a heritage from the Lord, children a reward from him." Children have value, and the God of heaven and earth gives them to us to treasure.

Instead of a baby in a toilet, imagine a dad lovingly putting his arms around his child, smiling warmly at the upturned face, and saying, "I often thank our Lord for giving you as a special gift to me. You are one of my greatest treasures."

How does that make a child feel?

Fortunately, few children are in danger of being left in a cardboard box. But many never feel a father's arms hugging them. They never see the smile of delight in a dad's heart. They hear criticism, rejection, and condemnation. No wonder they can hardly wait to get out of the house, hibernating meanwhile in their rooms, where they feel safe.

Adults who are otherwise upright, law-abiding citizens think nothing of communicating low esteem to their children. They would never consider killing an infant. But there are other ways to destroy life.

Words kill. "The tongue has the power of life and death, and those who love it will eat its fruit" (Proverbs 18:21). Adults who would never harm a child physically make a habit of destroying a teenager's self-image with verbal attacks as devastating as a sword thrust: sarcasm; criticism; mockery; verbal threats; put-down jokes; humiliation; condemnation.

Our Lord places high value on each life. He instructs us in Ephesians 4:29 to use words that strengthen and build. Nowhere is this more important than in family communication. Even when a child struggles and fails, that child needs to know someone values him, someone will treat her with respect. Unconditional love accompanies actions with words of gladness and value toward our children.

What's your child worth? How can you let your child know today?

Father, it's easy to speak carelessly to our children.
May Your Spirit remind us that we are guardians
of our words and of young lives in our care.

FATHER FIGURES

*Ruth says those of us who were off traveling missed the
best part of our lives—enjoying the children as they grew.
She is probably right.*
—Billy Graham (*Just as I Am*[18])

*After this, Jesus and his disciples went out into
the Judean countryside, where he spent
some time with them, and baptized.*
John 3:22

In 1996 the Gallup organization joined with the National
Center for Fathering to conduct a survey of both men and
women that might discover how today's dads fulfill their
fathering roles.

The results of the survey were sometimes surprising.
Although we men generally rate ourselves well at fatherhood, our wives (and the mothers of our children) often
have a different opinion.

For example, more than nine out of ten dads (92 percent) said they "have a good handle on how a child's needs change over childhood." In spite of that male self-confidence, only about seven of ten moms agreed with dads on that point.

Nine of ten dads said they "often do things together" with their children. But if the moms are to be believed, about one in five of those dads are lying. Only 73 percent of the moms said their children often do things together with dad.[19]

There are a few things both parents agree on, however. Of all the people surveyed, 90 percent agreed with the statement, "Fathers make unique contributions to their children's lives."

We're at least beginning to recognize that truth. In fact, in another survey, three out of four men (75 percent) said they would trade rapid career advancement for the chance to have more time with their families. Nearly one in three (30 percent) reported putting that attitude into action by personally turning down a job promotion or transfer that would have reduced time with family.

In addition, more than 90 percent of dads today are present for their children's births, up from a paltry 27 percent in 1974. And a study of federal agencies using "flex time" showed that more than half of the fathers there chose to come to work early in order to go home earlier and spend more time with family.[20]

All of these statistics about fathers boil down to time. Your absence from your family—physical, emotional, or spiritual—hinders your ability to transfer joy to your children. Likewise, when you buck the trend and commit to simply being there for your kids, you lay a foundation on which joy can be built.

You will always have work; you won't always have preschoolers, or elementary kids, or junior high and high schoolers running in and out of your doors. Make the choice to spend enough time with your kids that your wife would respond with an enthusiastic "Yes!" to the question "Do your children and their father often do things together?"

Dear Jesus, please remind me that joyful love can often be spelled t-i-m-e.

MAJOR LEAGUE DAD

That man will never be unwelcome to others
who makes himself agreeable to his own family.
—Plautus

If anyone does not provide for his relatives,
and especially for his immediate family,
he has denied the faith and is worse than an unbeliever.
1 Timothy 5:8

What kid hasn't dreamed of being a major league base-ball star? . . .leading the league in home runs. . . hurling a no-hitter. . .playing in the World Series. . .being chosen to play in the All-Star Game. . .having a baseball card and lots of people hollering, "Sign my baseball!"

Tim Burke lived some of that dream. Then he moved to new heights as a major league dad.[21]

Tim and Christine were married while he was pursuing the dream of being a major league pitcher. Their early years of marriage were spent traveling the minor league circuit, waiting for the big opportunity. They also dreamed of building a family. But this hope had a shocking setback the day their doctor told them that they would probably never be able to conceive a child.

So they changed their focus to pursue adoption. By the time Tim made it to the major leagues, an opportunity came to adopt a Korean-born infant. They named her Stephanie. When they began to think about adopting again, their thoughts turned to children with special needs. They choose an infant boy from a Guatemalan orphanage and named him Ryan. Ryan had mental retardation and would require special care.

Then the adoption agency told them of a Korean child born without a right hand and with a malfunctioning heart. Tim and Christine became convinced that the Lord wanted them to have this special child. She became their Nicole, a child who would need heart surgery and much love and care. They discovered that Nicole, like Ryan, had mental retardation. She also had thirty or forty epileptic seizures a day.

Tim's baseball career had been flourishing during these years. In 1989, while he was with the Montreal Expos, he had been chosen to pitch in an All-Star Game, one of baseball's highest honors. By the spring of 1993 he was at the top of his career, making lots of money and ready for spring training with the Cincinnati Reds. But an inner tension was pulling him to spend more time with Christine and his children.

That February 27 he went into his manager's office and said, "I've decided to retire." The manager was shocked, but Tim's decision was firm.

Reporters quizzed Tim about his decision. He responded: "My family needs me more than the Reds do. Baseball's going to do just fine without me, but I'm the only father my children have. I'm the only husband my wife has. And they need me now."

In our book Tim Burke is an All-Star dad. "I'm the only father my children have." That's major league thinking.

You'll learn more about Tim Burke in the fascinating book he wrote with his wife, *Major League Dad,* available from Focus on the Family Publishing.

Heavenly Father, make me a major league dad!

BALLOT BLOOPERS

Most people are about as happy as
they make up their minds to be.
—Abraham Lincoln

This is the day the Lord has made;
let us rejoice and be glad in it.
Psalm 118:24

An election is serious business. Many wars have been fought to gain voting rights. Black Americans and women of all races had to fight long and hard to gain this franchise. No other action so characterizes a free society. Elections are also big business. In the United States alone there are more than a half million elective offices. Politicians spend billions of dollars in an election year.

Still, it's worth noting that elections can be frightfully funny enterprises. Consider:

❖ In 1938 in Milton, Washington, Boston Curtis was elected Republican precinct committee-man. The problem was that Boston Curtis was the mayor's mule. The mayor, a Democrat, had filed for his mule—complete with hoofprint signature—to show the carelessness of voters.

❖ In Sweden's 1985 parliamentary elections, Donald Duck received a respectable 291 votes. Mr. Potato Head only received four votes for mayor of Boise, Idaho.

❖ Running for U.S. Senate in 1950, George Smathers sent out mailers charging that his opponent, Claude Pepper, was a "practicing homosapien" (human being) and stating that Pepper's sister was a known "thespian" (actress). Pepper had, he alleged, "matricu-lated" (graduated from school) with young women. What could Pepper do? The allegations were true. Smathers won.

❖ The 1948 Democratic Convention organizers wanted dozens of pigeons to fly dramatically past a flower sculpture of the Liberty Bell during a speech. On cue the cages were opened—but the birds wouldn't fly until workers tossed them into the air. Then they perched in the rafters and dropped "comments" on the proceedings.

❖ Among parties active over the years in Britain:
The-Ban-the-Old-Fogies Party, The Jim-the-Fish
Conservative Independent Party, The Nobody
Party, The Raving Loony Society of Cambridge,
and The Best-Party-I've-Ever-Been-To Party.

❖ Luther Knox legally changed his name to
"None of the Above" in his bid for Louisiana's
governorship in 1979.

❖ Louis Abalofia once ran for U.S. President with
the slogan, "I have nothing to hide." His cam-
paign flyers featured a full-length picture of
Mr. Abalofia—nude.

If humor can be found in so serious a subject as an
election, certainly there is happiness to be discovered in
your daily life. Today is the day to capture those moments
of joy. Share them with your children.

*Lord God, make the joyful moments in my life
sparkle like precious gems today.*

MEMORIES ARE MADE OF THIS

*Many families have more to live on
than they have to live for.*
—Anonymous

*He who gets wisdom loves his own soul;
he who cherishes understanding prospers.*
Proverbs 19:8

Norm was in the seminary library looking for a great find in the duplicate volumes the library was giving away. That's when he noticed an old friend, an exposition of the Book of Revelation.

"Immediately my mind flashed back over forty years to when I was reading that book and had gained a valuable insight that fastened itself in my mind. That one truth had stuck fast in my memory.

"I thought about other memories that had attached themselves to my mind. I've never forgotten the Saturday nights when I was in the third grade. Mom and Dad would go to the movies and leave us four boys at home. I resented having to go to bed earlier than my brothers. After I was upstairs in bed (or so they thought), they listened to the radio program 'Gangbusters.' Each program featured the life and just fate of some criminal. It was scary—and fun.

"I'd stretch out on the floor with my ear to the heating duct, spellbound at the unfolding drama. At the conclusion of the program the announcer would say, 'Be on the lookout for Dangerous Dan Corrigan who is on the loose and may be in your neighborhood. He is armed and considered dangerous.' I'd crawl into bed then, fearful and trembling, certain that Dangerous Dan was just outside the window.

"I can't remember my third-grade teacher's name, but 'Dangerous Dan Corrigan' remains fresh in my mind to this day."

Our children are compiling their own memory scrapbooks. We have an unparalleled opportunity to help them experience memories they will cherish forever. We can find great delight in providing fun and meaningful life experiences that will give strength to their lives and hope for their futures.

Norm recalls a conversation with a man in his forties who said he had completely missed his adolescent years, strung out on drugs and alcohol. Those years were a blur. He never experienced a healthy adolescence, and that loss left him with an inner sadness.

The wise father creates an enriched environment in which his child can taste the wonder of life. He opens the larger world to his sons and daughters and walks along with them, sharing the events and becoming part of the memories. This rich storehouse of remembering will be a place where that person can find strength, laughter, and joy.

Dear Jesus, show me how to make the joy
You provide a vivid memory in the childhood
my young ones are experiencing today.

THINGS YOU DIDN'T KNOW YOU DIDN'T KNOW!

Impossible things are happening every day.
—Cinderella's fairy godmother
(Rodgers and Hammerstein's *Cinderella*)

With God all things are possible.
Matthew 19:26

D id you know:

- ❖ There are as many chickens as there are humans? Dogs live to be about twelve years old, cats make it to fifteen, goldfish to seventeen, and a deep sea clam can live to 100?
- ❖ Your brain will store more than one million bits of information in an average year?
- ❖ Olympic champion swimmers swim about five miles an hour, while the sailfish cruises at

about sixty-eight miles an hour?

❖ In ancient Arabia, people could sometimes get tax exemptions by bathing regularly?

❖ Pluto was discovered using a reflector made from the crankshaft of a 1910 Buick?

❖ A professionally spiked volleyball goes about eighty miles an hour? Bert Loomis invented the basketball dribble? A golf ball has 336 dimples? There are about 141,000 tennis courts in the U.S.?

❖ Girl babies smile more than boy babies? Fish sunburn? Short men live longer than tall men? Chances are one in nineteen that you have red hair?

❖ The first doughnut with a hole was invented in 1847?

❖ The 1896 war between Great Britain and Zanzibar lasted thirty-eight minutes?

❖ The fastest clocked time for making a bed is 17.3 seconds?

❖ In Germany, you can buy artificial, spray-on dirt to make your car look like you drove it off-road? In Canada it is illegal to enter a plane while it is in flight?

❖ In Taiwan, a study learned that people eat lunch because they're hungry? The U.S. government once spent $46,000 to find out how long it takes to cook breakfast?

❖ Ben Franklin invented the rocking chair? Mark Twain invented suspenders? Thomas Edison invented the lightbulb, movies, and cement furniture? Wolfgang Mozart composed "Twinkle, Twinkle, Little Star"?

❖ Wasps are nearsighted? An elephant drinks fifty gallons of water a day? A mole can tunnel the length of a football field in one day?

❖ The Chinese wore sunglasses as early as the sixth century?

❖ You'll walk about 65,000 miles before you die?

❖ In Washington, D.C., there are more telephones than people?

❖ In 1439 King Henry VI banned kissing?

❖ William Tyndale was executed for translating the Bible into English?

❖ Thirty-eight percent of Americans sing in the shower?

❖ Taking time to enjoy life and your kids is not an impossible task?

Now you know.

Heavenly Father, help me to know You more, for only in knowing You can I know true joy.

LESSON FROM
A CRANKY DAD

All you need to grow fine,
vigorous grass is a crack in your sidewalk.
—Will Rogers

You were taught, with regard to your former way of life,
to put off your old self, which is being corrupted
by its deceitful desires; to be made new
in the attitude of your minds.
Ephesians 4:22–23

You don't wake up in the morning, flip on the light switch, and suddenly feel joyful. If you have young children, you may flip on a light and feel downright cranky from a lack of sleep. Mike had such an experience recently:

"Our very best family friends came over for a weekend, and (as usual) we stayed up way too late talking and playing games. The next morning we were dragging out of bed—except the kids, of course. Our children were unending bundles of energy, plus there weren't enough bathrooms, no one felt like making breakfast, and none of us had ironed clothes for church.

"Lying exhausted in bed, I could hear the rising din of kids who'd gotten up at the crack of dawn and who would rather play than dress. Mixed in were sounds of parents who'd rather sleep than eat. I groaned. Suddenly, I realized that this day was mine. I didn't have to be a poster-child for the Crankiness Foundation; nor did anyone else.

"Although I didn't believe it at first, I dragged out of bed and announced to my wife, 'Today is going to be a great day.' She didn't believe it either. 'Why is that?' she snapped. Smiling, I shrugged and said, 'It just is. I've got a good feeling about it.' A half-smile played on her lips as she looked me in the eyes and said, 'Maybe you're right.'

"Encouraged, I looked for my friends and the rest of my family. One by one I made the announcement that this would be a good day. The children already knew it. One adult friend seemed relieved, saying, 'I'm so glad.'

"The tension eased. A few smiles broke out. Sure, we were late for church, but so what? After all, today was going to be a great day. And you know, it turned out even better than I expected."

Rather than give in to a joyless Sunday morning, Mike chose to plant a seed of joy into the lives of those in his house. All he did really was to change his own attitude, but that was enough to infect those around him and change the mood.

Are you a father who plants bits of joy into the rooms of your home? As the father goes, so goes the family—especially when it comes to setting an emotional climate at home. "Dad's in a bad mood" means everyone must stay out of his way. "For some reason, Dad's got a smile on his face today" frees the rest of the family to smile, too.

It would be nice if we could shove responsibility for creating happy memories onto other family members, but that's not the way life is. A mother makes an irreplaceable contribution to a family's legacy, and siblings wield a strong influence on the way childhood memories are shaped. But it's the father who leads, who sets the tone, who must initiate and cultivate a legacy of joy. When have your seen your attitude affect the attitudes of those in your family? What have you done with that power?

Lord, I need a new attitude.
Please help me to choose joy each day this week.

PROGRESS REPORT

People liked being with Jesus; where he was, joy was.
—Philip Yancey (*The Jesus I Never Knew*[22])

*Be diligent in these matters; give yourself wholly to them,
so that everyone may see your progress.*
1 Timothy 4:15

Floating around the internet recently was a list of quotes from employee performance evaluations and progress reports:

- ❖ "Since my last report, this employee has reached rock bottom—and has started to dig."
- ❖ "His men would follow him anywhere, but only out of morbid curiosity."
- ❖ "I would not allow this employee to breed."
- ❖ "This associate is really not so much of a has-been; more of a definitely-won't-be."

- ❖ "[This employee] works well when under constant supervision and cornered like a rat in a trap."
- ❖ "Whenever she opens her mouth, it seems that this is only to change whichever foot was previously in there."
- ❖ "He would be out of his depth in a parking lot puddle."
- ❖ "This young lady has delusions of adequacy."
- ❖ "He sets low personal standards and then consistently fails to achieve them."
- ❖ "This employee is depriving a village somewhere of an idiot."
- ❖ "This employee should go far—and the sooner the better."

We chuckle at these if only because they could have described us at some point. Every employee is required to have some kind of regular progress report. Every student must endure periodic evaluation. Even politicians are graded at election time. For some reason fathers have gotten off the hook. No one writes a performance evaluation or gives us a progress report on how we're doing at passing along joy.

So, in the interest of fairness, here's our "Joyful Father" evaluation for you (and us!):

"This father sincerely wants to be a man who imparts joyful, happy memories to his children. In many ways, he's succeeding. Here are goals we'd suggest this father pursue for the next quarter:

"*Pray more.* Sometimes this dad depends too much on his own strength. He needs to remember that the source of eternal joy, Jesus, is constantly at his side, able and willing to help.

"*Relax more.* Life isn't always as serious as this father makes it out to be.

"*Spend more time.* This father can't enjoy his children if he never sees them.

"*Laugh more.* Joy is catching. This father needs to be a carrier."

Someday your children will write your true progress report with their lives and memories. Live today so that report will recommend you for a raise.

Dear Jesus, please enable me to pray more,
relax more, spend more time, and
laugh more in the months that come.

BUSINESS BEFORE BUSINESS

I just enjoy being out with my kids!
—Steve Camp

Their children will see it and be joyful;
their hearts will rejoice in the Lord.
Zechariah 10:7

Christian musician Steve Camp had every reason to go to work. His record company had scheduled a meeting to discuss his new recording contract. Big dollars and prestige hinged on the outcome of that negotiation.

But Steve refused to attend the meeting at that time and asked that it be rescheduled. "I have a very important meeting that's going to take up the basis of that afternoon," he told the company executives.

They rescheduled, and all went well. But knowing what was at stake in this contract, the record executives were curious. At the meeting, he was asked about that important meeting that had taken priority over them.

Steve told them matter-of-factly that he had promised to spend that afternoon playing with his kids. No high-dollar contract was going to break that commitment.

That kind of commitment to family is the soil in which we plant seeds of joy. It's a commitment that says, "Next to my relationship with Jesus Christ, nothing in this life has a higher priority than do you."

Commitment to family begins in commitment to wife. Not every father has the benefit of raising children in partnership with a wife. Those of you that do need to hear Josh McDowell's advice on fathering: "The greatest thing a father can do for his children is to love their mother."

There is immense security for children in knowing that no matter what happens, mom and dad will always love, support, and be there for each other.

Do your happy childhood memories include your father, mother, or both parents?

What do they tell you about your dad?

What do they suggest about your daily planner?

Lord Jesus, grant me wisdom to recognize—
and properly set priorities—
around the priceless moments I have
with my children this week.

LET US PLAY

"Let's play catch, Daddy.
I'll pitch the ball and you say 'Good throw!'"
—"Family Circus" cartoon

However many years a man may live,
let him enjoy them all.
Ecclesiastes 11:8

"Okay, I'll admit it," says Mike. "When my wife asked our four-year-old son what he liked best about dad, I half-hoped he'd shout, 'He's the smartest dad in the world!' Or better, 'He's the strongest dad alive!'

"Instead, Tony gave a greater compliment. 'I like best about my dad,' he said after a moment's thought, 'that he plays with me.'

"I had thought kneeling among his collection of toys was just another 'dad duty.' Now I realize it's a *privilege.* And I've discovered play can open doors for faith development and leave a legacy of joy."

So how can a father make the most of play? Here are a few suggestions:

Ignite the imagination using Scripture as the spark. David and Goliath is Tony's favorite Bible story, so for a birthday party we used homemade toys and played games with that story's theme. A dozen little ones were thrilled to fling toy slings toward a menacing "Goliath" target. We've used Bible action figures to play "What if. . . ?" What if Peter had faced Goliath? What if you and I were threatened by the fiery furnace instead of Shadrach, Meshach, and Abednego? We add silly voices to portray good guys and bad guys and throw in a few obstacles—such as the Couch Cliff and Piano Bench Cave.

Keep it simple. Don't cover "The Four Spiritual Laws" each time you pull out a Christian toy. Don't feel compelled to discuss theology over Mary and Esther dolls. Avoid being preachy or complicated or inflexible. Spark interests without excess baggage. You can focus on the relationship and let rules be secondary. It's the relationship that earns trust, which allows you to speak at the right time about faith in Jesus.

Demonstrate enthusiasm. Whether it's playing a new CD-ROM game on the computer or dressing up in sheets to play "Joseph and Mary Go to Bethlehem," show by example that it's okay to have fun. Your actions tell your child that faith in Jesus is accompanied by joy. Enthusiastic participation says that you value time with your child and that he or she is an equal partner in your play.

Make play a priority. In Mike's house, after dinner is typically "family time." Everyone—parent and child alike—puts aside demands of the day and focuses on playing and hanging out together. Sometimes the family plays board games; other times they play with action figures or in the backyard. It really doesn't matter what happens, as long as there is a commitment to doing it.

"During those after-dinner times," says Mike, "I remember what I like best about my son. It's that he plays with me, too."

Lord Jesus, remind me
to add three important words
to my vocabulary today:
Let's play games!

PRE-GAME RITUALS

I fondly recall many family rituals, a number of which were centered around the dinner table. Dinner itself was a sort of ritual.
—Anne Fillin[23]

The plans of the diligent lead to profit.
Proverbs 21:5

"Patrick wasn't amused."

A teammate of NBA superstar Patrick Ewing had noticed that every night before a Knicks' game, Pat would sit in the locker room and dribble a ball, using the same cadence over and over again.

"Once, I thought it would be funny to knock the ball away," says the anonymous teammate. He won't do that again. Professional athletes have almost religious devotion to their rituals.

Mario Elie wants to be sure his adrenaline is flowing

come game time, so he insists that equipment manager, David Nordstrom, curse him out each night in the locker room.

Each night when the national anthem was playing, Celtic legend Larry Bird would lock his eyes on hockey great Bobby Orr's retired jersey hanging from the rafters.

For years, Danny Ferry of the Cleveland Cavaliers has brought a stack of books to the arena before each game. To the puzzlement of teammates, he takes that stack and, fully clothed, goes into the showers for about fifteen minutes. He has never explained his behavior.

Derek Harper of the Orlando Magic has a more physical ritual. He arrives hours before a game and plunges right into a whirlpool, then receives a body massage, takes a nap, exercises on a stationary bicycle, applies heat packs, stretches out, mixes a nutritional drink for his game-time water bottle, and then jogs out to play.

Derek's teammate, Penny Hardaway, doesn't work quite that hard, but he's certainly cleaner. Penny refuses to play a game in any piece of clothing that got sweaty during warm-ups, so he often changes uniforms before a game.

Kevin Johnson, long known as a model Christian witness for the Phoenix Suns, is diligent to go to chapel before each game—and to brush his teeth.

Although you may chuckle at these practices, you have to admire players' willingness to pay diligent attention to the smallest details they think will enhance their performances. Imagine how our fatherhood would change if we practiced similar devotion toward the daily rituals that add joy to relationships with our kids.

If we always strove to have dinner as a family. . . . If we set aside one Saturday a month for "family-only" activities. . . . If we took one evening a week to study the Bible, pray, and share with our children. . . . If we greeted our children each morning with a smile—no matter how little sleep we got the night before.

And if, when someone or something tried to interfere with our family rituals, we let them know that we, like Patrick Ewing, were not amused by the intrusion.

Jesus, give me an athlete's diligence
to invest in the little family rituals
that build my relationships with my children.

WATCH OUT FER THEM MOSQUITOES!

My grandparents told me that I was special,
and they told me it so much that I started believing it.
—Kevin Johnson, Phoenix Suns

Children's children are a crown to the aged,
and parents are the pride of their children.
Proverbs 17:6

When Norm was a child, he jumped with excitement at the words, "Get in the back of the truck. We're going over to your grandpa and grandma's for the day."

Their house was an oasis of joy in the midst of the emotional desert of Norm's home. Norm's dad never smiled, joked, or played with his children. The common statements at home were: "Keep out of my way," "Now you're in trouble," and "I haven't got time for your foolishness."

Grandma and Grandpa Learn's house radiated with warmth and cheer. The house itself was plain and simple. The siding on the outside had never been finished, and the inside furnishings were well worn. What made it special was Norm's grandparents.

"I always looked forward to Grandpa's sense of humor. It fired any young boy's heart. One special ritual that always sparked his creative imagination usually took place in the evening when we'd be sitting on the front porch of the farmhouse. He'd be rocking in his rocking chair with a chaw of tobacco in his mouth.

" 'Did I ever tell you about the big mosquitoes we used to have around here before you was born?' He'd say it with a twinkle in his eyes. Then off he went on his imaginative tale. "One night I woke up hearing a grinding sound. I peeked out the window and saw a bunch of them sharpening their beaks on the grindstone outside the house. Their beaks were about a foot long. What d'ya think of that?'

" 'Once I was outside working when three or four of them critters came after me. I grabbed a metal tub and put it over my head to protect me. Them mosquitoes dove after me and run their beaks right through that tub. Quick as a flash I grabbed a hammer and bent their beaks over. They flew off carrying that tub with them. They was big critters!'

" 'Now Fay,' chimed in Grandma, 'you shouldn't be

filling that child's head with silly nonsense.' But she was happy her husband cared so much for his grandchildren. She was well aware of our unhappy home life and wanted to see her grandchildren cared for."

Grandpa Learn was a ray of hope for a lonely, mixed-up young boy who was ignored and rejected by a busy, unhappy father.

"With my grandfather I was treated as someone special. I doubt that he realized what an impression he left on me. He was a poor farmer—poor financially and poor in farming skill—but he was a master at relating to his grandson. He passed on a heritage of joy that I've been able to reinvest in my children—and grandchildren! By example he taught me that it's never foolish to connect with my kids."

Have you been a bit foolish with a child lately? It might be a wise—and lasting—investment in his or her life.

Holy Spirit, please inspire a foolish moment
with my children for me today.

WHAT THEY DID RIGHT

Looking back, it seems that my parents did many things right, even though at the time right was the last word I would have used to describe some of their actions.
—Beatrice[24]

In everything set them an example by doing what is good.
Titus 2:7

What will our sons and daughters remember about us when they become adults? What will they recall that we did right? Or wrong? What stories will they pass on to the next generation about us?

Some years ago adults were invited to submit chapters to a book entitled *What They Did Right*. Some individuals declined because they couldn't recall any positive actions by their parents. One response to the editor's request was, "Too bad you're not asking what they did wrong! I could write about that." But listen to the memories men and women shared that attest to "what they did right."

❖ I think I grew to love the Lord because I loved my father, and you just couldn't separate the two.—David Gill

❖ One of the ways our parents helped us to develop strong self-images was by creating a strong family unit.—Deborah Bayly

❖ I learned to understand the nature of faith in God by observing their lives.—Jonathan Baylis

❖ One of my earliest memories is of running into a barbed-wire fence when I was about three. Father gathered me into his arms and tenderly thanked God that I hadn't been injured. He is a tender man, and it is a tenderness not from his upbringing but from his constant converse with God.—J. E. Runions

❖ We are, all six of us, unspeakably grateful that we were taught authority, acceptance, the arts of listening and observation, and the necessity of biblical order. Beyond this, we were loved.—Elisabeth Elliot

❖ When I first began to think about "what they did right," their appreciation for us as individuals with different gifts stood out most in my mind.—Dawn Frasieur

❖ My dad's sense of humor colored much of his thinking. His gentle aphorisms enabled him to get his point across to us children effectively as well as inoffensively.—Betty Bube

❖ As I look back I'm aware of the tremendous influence he had on my life, yet I can think of very few times when he lectured me.—Donald Miller

❖ The person who most influenced me in my childhood was certainly my father. . . . He treated me as an intelligent person. . . . He always upheld his authority, but he showed us great tenderness.—Jean Sutherland

These individuals received a priceless legacy from their fathers who are a past generation. Today is our opportunity to invest in the future—the lives of our children—and leave behind a legacy in their lives. What will we do right?

Dear Lord, grant me the wisdom to do
something right in the life of my child today
and so make a happy memory for tomorrow.

WHO'S YOUR FAVORITE?

"Dear God, What is the rest of the story about when you made boys and girls? There must be a reason why you made two different brands of people."
—Hank, age 6[25]

For God does not show favoritism.
Romans 2:11

An assignment for a course in marriage and family studies demanded that a father log and analyze the time spent with family members over a six-week period. One father looked over the data and realized that he spent more time with his sons than with his daughter.

"I am certain that I love her as much as I do the boys, but I think that I was unconsciously drawn to the boys because of my conditioning. I was sending Susan a message that she was less important than the boys. So I determined to correct that imbalance and seek ways to spend quality time with her. Thus far I'm doing quite well and she said that she enjoys our father/daughter times a lot."

A study at the University of Washington found that fathers with only daughters spend less time with their children. Gender made little difference with the mothers.

Researchers pointed out that men often feel uncomfortable in non-male activities. Our daughters notice that discomfort. Dandi Daley Mackall asked children to describe "the world's greatest dad." One youngster replied, "He'd whip all the bullies and fling them to high heaven." A young daughter added, "The greatest dad would play girl games, too."[26]

A wise dad recognizes the crucial role he plays in a daughter's development. He is her first impression of masculinity, the model of her future husband, the shaper of her self-image as a woman, the model by which she evaluates men, and the shaper of her view of her heavenly Father.

Mark pursues a high-quality relationship with his daughter, Becky. He joined a father/daughter club with other like-minded men. They plan activities meaningful to both fathers and daughters. Reflecting on his experience, Mark noted, "The men I know are very busy. Unless we schedule these times for fun, loving interactions, they aren't likely to happen. Some men say they envy the relationship I have with Becky, but I tell them they could have it with their daughters if they wanted to. I'm glad I started doing this when she was young."

Norm recalls an event that occurred over twenty years ago:

"I was speaking at a conference on family life. The worship leader was a robust, joyful man who energized the audience. His daughter was visiting during a break in her college studies. As he introduced her, she came and stood at his side. I'll never forget the warm smile on her face as she looked at her father. It communicated love and admiration. As a father of four young daughters at the time, I was challenged to pursue that kind of relationship with my children."

If you had to evaluate your time with your daughters, what grade would you make?

Holy Father, help me to be a father
to my children like You are a Father to me.

ON FOOTBALLS AND FATHERS

*It is actually quite easy to throw a perfect football spiral—
provided your child is six foot three, 245 pounds, with
giant hands and upper body strength.*
—John Boswell and Ron Barrett (*How to Dad*[27])

*Hope deferred makes the heart sick,
but a longing fulfilled is a tree of life.*
Proverbs 13:12

Jesse Butterworth was not one to spout a list a mile long
when it came time for presents. No, this thoughtful, soon-
to-be six-year-old weighed his options conscientiously,
planned his future play time well, and asked only for the
things he really wanted.

When it came time to plan his sixth birthday party,
Jesse instructed his parents to hold the party at a certain
place, to invite particular friends, to provide a definite menu,
and to acquire a specific cake. With all this deliberation, it's

no surprise Jesse had certain birthday gifts in mind. Jesse's dad, Bill, finally broached the subject, asking what presents he wanted for his upcoming birthday.

"Dad," Jesse replied carefully. "I'd like a ball to play with for my birthday."

"Great," Bill responded. "What kind of ball do you want?"

"I think I'd like either a football or a soccer ball."

"OK," said Bill, pressing for more details. "Which would you like more, a football or a soccer ball?"

There was a pause. Then with a wisdom beyond his years, Jesse said, "We-e-e-e-l-l-l-l-l-l. . . If you had some time to play ball with me this next year, I'd really like a football for you and me to throw around in the backyard. But if you're gonna be real busy again this year, maybe you just better get me a soccer ball, because I can play soccer with the rest of the kids in the neighborhood."

Bill realized then that Jesse wasn't really asking for a ball for his birthday. He was asking for his dad.

The thing this almost-first-grader wanted most was simply to enjoy some time with his father—to be important enough to rate a game or two in the backyard with Dad, to make the "A-list" in Dad's schedule.

Though your kids might not be able to say it as did Jesse, what they really want most from you is you. They want to be a part of your life, to laugh with you, to play with you, to rate as one of your highest priorities. They want to enjoy you and want you to enjoy them back.

Bill mumbled an "OK, I'll surprise you on your birthday," to Jesse, and left to make his plans for the party.

Bill Butterworth later reported that "The oddest thing occurred on my son's sixth birthday. It's a moment we'll never forget—a grown man and a little boy embracing and sobbing tears of joy. All over a dumb old football."[28]

*Dear Father, give me the wisdom and
the opportunity to enjoy my children today.*

THREE BLIND STORIES

If I'd known I was going to live this long,
I'd have taken better care of myself.
—George Burns

One thing I do know. I was blind but now I see!
John 9:25

American League umpire Jack Kerns was used to player grumbling. Every umpire has been called "blind" or worse. Still, those terms took new meaning during a game Kerns umpired in the 1950s.

Although the game was running late into the evening, Kerns refused to stop play on account of darkness. In the bottom of the ninth inning, the pitcher and catcher could barely see the ball—even though they knew where it was going. When the last batter on the opposing team got two strikes, the pitcher and catcher called time-out to devise a plan.

Instead of risking another throw, the pitcher secretly

handed off the ball to the catcher. The pitcher went through his normal windup and then elaborately pantomimed his pitch. The catcher popped his mitt in the strike zone, pretending to catch the ball.

"Strike three and out!" Kerns yelled with confidence. The opposing player immediately objected. Fuming at the umpire, he turned and shouted, "Strike? You blind (expletive)! That ball was two feet outside!"[29]

Blindness isn't limited to sports. Consider the American who almost invented the vacuum cleaner. It was 1901, and the American genius had created a "carpet-dust-removing machine," a small boxed engine with a bag that blew dust off a carpet. A British man, Hubert Cecil Booth, saw the invention demonstrated and was intrigued. He approached the American and suggested, "It should suck air, not blow it."

The deeply offended American scoffed at the impossible idea and stormed away. So Booth went home, made the modifications himself, and invented a staple of modern life.[30]

Could you be somehow blind, too? Let's find out. In the space at the end of this chapter, draw the details of the face on your watch—without looking at your watch for a reference.

Now, compare your drawing to the real thing. How'd you do? You probably missed a small decoration, the second hand, or the name of the watch-making company printed on the face. How could you be blind to something you look at a dozen times or more a day?

Scientists call it being "homeblind." Commonplace details fail to register. You could do the same experiment with a penny, your wife's face, a tie you are wearing. You are "homeblind" to the familiar. And sometimes we fathers become homeblind to the precious joy our children provide and possess.

Remember how you felt the first time you held your infant child? Remember the miracle? The rush of relief and joyful exhilaration?

You still hold that precious child, only now the child can hold you back. Don't be blind to the joy that brings.

Father, open my eyes to the
miracle my children are today.

OPPORTUNISTIC FATHERING

Somehow, we must learn how to achieve momentary
slowdowns, and request from God a heightened
awareness of the conception that life is a happy thing.
—Luci Swindoll
(*You Bring the Confetti, God Brings the Joy*[31])

What has happened to all your joy?
Galatians 4:15

You can't always predict when the opportunity to create a happy memory will present itself. But you can always be on the lookout for those special moments.

Mrs. McGrath didn't miss an opportunity to create a happy memory for her husband. A horrible snowstorm blanketed the Chicago area. Mrs. McGrath had gone into the garage for a few boxes. Moments later there was a crash. The snow-burdened garage roof had collapsed—with Mrs. McGrath inside.

Grabbing a snow shovel, Mr. McGrath raced outside, yelling for neighbors to help. Without a coat or gloves, Robert began digging furiously, tossing snow, pulling debris out. Sweat froze on his body, but he refused to give up until he finally had reached his wife. Sobbing with joy, he kept asking, "Are you all right?"

She was unharmed. In fact, she hadn't even been in the garage when it collapsed. She had gone in one door of the garage, and out the other. She was inside the house when she heard her husband yelling to neighbors and saw him frantically digging through the rubble to rescue her. So, she put on her coat, sneaked back into the garage, and waited for her husband to pull her out from under the caved-in roof. She let herself be rescued so her husband could feel the joy of being a hero.

You may not get (or want) a chance to have your children pull you out from under a pile of snow and timber, but like Mrs. McGrath, you can make your kids feel like heroes as long as you have an opportunistic attitude.

When you take time to read a book to your pre-schooler, you've demonstrated that you value him more than the evening news you were reading. He feels as important as a hero. When you take your daughter out for ice cream—for no reason at all—you've demonstrated that you like who she is and who she's becoming. You've made her feel admired like a hero.

When you show up for your junior-higher's sporting events, theater presentations, and music recitals, you've communicated that he or she is worth watching. You've helped that child perform like a hero.

And when you wrap your arms around your high school son and hug him each day, you tell him that your love is stronger than the embarrassment that can come between men showing affection. You've given him a hero's welcome.

You can always find at least one excuse for planting joy in your child's life each day. It's as simple as being an opportunistic dad, always on the lookout for the right moment.

Dear God, help me build joyful heroes
out of the giggly children in my life.

A HERITAGE OF FAITH

Years from now, they'll remember you by
what they see in your kids.
—Bill Butterworth (*My Kids Are My Best Teachers*)

Your love, O Lord, reaches to the heavens,
your faithfulness to the skies.
Psalm 36:5

She was a student at Westmont College, struggling to make ends meet. Now she huddled with her friends in an intimate circle of mutual friendship. The discussion drifted toward financial pressures each of them was feeling.

"I went to the post office, and the only mail I had was my monthly financial statement from the college," she said. "Every time I see the amount I owe, I get anxious. I don't have the resources to supply what the college wants.

"But then a peace settles into my soul. I know everything is going to be okay, and I know why it happens that way. My parents are missionaries to a tribe of Native Americans. They have served for years in what is called a 'faith mission.' The missionaries are to trust our Lord for needs. You're almost looked upon as unspiritual if you have too large a reserve.

"Many times my parents have faced a bill in the mail when they knew they couldn't pay what was due. Dad and Mom would spread out the bill and bow their heads in prayer. They would present the bill to the Lord. They were confident that He cared about this need and would look out for their interests.

"I saw that scene so many times it is ingrained in my mind. Now when I am in similar situations, I not only know what to do, but I know what will happen."

By passing on their Christian faith to this daughter, those missionary parents also passed on an ability to experience peace, no matter the circumstance. The Bible gives us a similar account of a faith being passed from generation to generation. The apostle Paul refers to it offhandedly to his protégé, Timothy. A sincere faith had lived in Timothy's grandmother, Lois, and then in his mother, Eunice. Now it lived in Timothy (2 Timothy 1:5).

We can visualize the godly woman, Lois, discovering that God is trustworthy and building a life rooted in His faithfulness. She lives out this abiding confidence in God in the presence of her daughter, Eunice. Eunice marries, and infant Timothy joins the household. The seeds of faith are sown, germinate, and grow deep into his heart. Young Tim receives the priceless heritage of faith.

Where will our children discover that their God is trustworthy? How will they find joyful peace in the midst of overwhelming circumstances? Who will verify in their own lives that people can stake their lives—and their joy—on His reliability?

We know the answer, don't we?

Holy Spirit, empower me to be an example
of joyful faith in action today.

LIVING WITH RISK

Did you hear about the fellow who went into business on a shoestring and tripled his investment? Now he's trying to figure out what to do with three shoestrings.
—Michael Hodgin

Without faith it is impossible to please God, because anyone who comes to him must believe that he exists and that he rewards those who earnestly seek him.
Hebrews 11:6

Norm's father lived to be ninety-two years old. But when he was in his late eighties, Norm's dad left a lesson that Norm still treasures:

"Dad and Mom had flown from Florida to visit us in Arizona. One day Dad and I talked about financial matters. This was not a normal topic of conversation; Dad was private about money. He mentioned the retirement funds that supplemented their social security. The interest on CDs and other secure investment opportunities was poor. So he and Mom had talked with a financial consultant. They could get a higher yield if they were willing to live with greater risk.

"Dad continued, 'I talked it over with your mother. We decided that we'd rather live with some reasonable risk and receive a decent return on our investment than to live with limited income because we couldn't accept any risk.'

"Dad gave me a wonderful gift that day. His example said, 'Son, don't be afraid to take a reasonable risk. Even at eighty-seven I'm not afraid to step out onto new ground.' I felt an indescribable joy that still brings inner gladness. My father is gone, but his legacy remains.

"I knew a woman in her eighties who couldn't live with risk. One day we were driving together through our neighborhood, noticing that buildings were being demolished so streets could be widened. 'I never like to see anything change,' my friend said. 'I feel more secure when everything stays as it is.' Everything about her life revealed what that attitude cost her. To the day she died she was fearful. She received almost no return on her investments because her rigidly guarded life ruled out laughter, joy, and adventure.

"Each year, my wife and I spend a week speaking at a family camp in the mountains above Colorado Springs. For years I watched individuals rappel a 130-foot cliff. Then one day I made the commitment. I was convinced that it was a reasonable challenge—not reckless foolishness.

The mountaineers gave thorough training.

"Then came the day of reckoning. As we climbed the trail to the peak, I was definitely in tune with my anxiety. As I backed off the 130-foot cliff, my fear made itself known. But I also was exhilarated. At the bottom I knew I had accomplished something I'd remember with joy.

"I want my children to remember me as a father who wasn't afraid to live with reasonable risks. I want them to know the joy of adventure, the joy of stepping out into the new and untried. Thanks, Dad, for showing me the way."

Lord Jesus, help me to not be afraid
of the risks my children need to learn joy.

SOMETHING TO THINK ABOUT, SOMETHING TO DO

Life affords no greater responsibility, no greater privilege,
than the raising of the next generation.
—C. Everett Koop[32]

The Lord has done great things for us,
and we are filled with joy.
Psalm 126:3

Congratulations! You're officially halfway through this book. With that in mind, we thought it might be good to take a moment now to reflect and apply some of the things we've discussed so far. We'll start with:

Something to Think About

❖ Fifteen years from now, how do you think your children will answer the question, "What one thing do you remember about your father from your childhood days?" How would you like them to remember you?

❖ What happy memories do you have from childhood? Do they include your father? Why or why not?

❖ Do you find it easy or difficult to have a joyful attitude? Why is this true?

❖ When have you seen your attitude impact the attitudes of those in your family?

❖ Would you most like to improve in: (1) unswerving commitment to your family, (2) an opportunistic attitude, or (3) determination? What can you do this week to grow in that area?

Something to Do

❖ Gather your family and brainstorm answers to this question: "What's an inexpensive family activity that everyone would enjoy?" Make a list of ideas, then have family members choose one. Arrange a time for your family to do that activity.

❖ Have family members each make a list titled, "Things that make me smile." (Older family members can help children unable to write.) When everyone has a list, take a camera and go on a "smile hunt," photographing things to represent every item on each list. If someone listed "pizza," you might photograph a local pizza parlor. Or, if someone listed "a hug from Mom," photograph a family hug session.

After you develop the film from your smile hunt, have the family gather to put the pictures in a special photo album. As you're arranging the pictures, have family members discuss what they could do to make sure that your family is always on a list of "things that make me smile."

Holy Father, thanks for giving me
the privilege of being a father like You.

MAKING MEMORIES STICK

I've learned that in every face-to-face encounter,
regardless of how brief, we leave something behind.
—a forty-five-year-old[33]

For whenever you eat this bread and drink this cup, you
proclaim the Lord's death until he comes.
1 Corinthians 11:26

Our Lord is responsible for starting many holidays. One of the most revered of Jewish holidays is the Passover. That holiday celebration is but one of many celebrations begun by a direct command of God. Here's how it came to be:

In ancient Egypt a momentous event is about to take place. God's people, enslaved in the land of Pharaoh, are going to be liberated, departing for a grand adventure! And God will personally fight the last battle to free them. The memory of this event will be precious to children for generations to come.

The death angel will pass over the land of Egypt, killing the firstborn child in each home. Every house that doesn't have the blood of a lamb on its door posts will be visited by that frightful angel. Heeding that warning, the Israelites sacrifice lambs and place the blood on their door posts. The Israelites don't lose one child.

But in the Egyptian homes, people wail through the night for their lost children. Pharaoh surrenders, sending Moses and the Israelites away. Victory has come for Moses and God's people!

But that's not the end. God wants His children to remember this battle, to remember how He rescued Israel from slavery. He doesn't command that a statue be chiseled or a mural depicting the battle be painted. He commands that His people party. He wants a holiday celebration. Each Israelite family is to celebrate a meal every year to remember this great deliverance. Moses tells the parents, "When your children ask you, 'What does this ceremony mean to you?' then tell them, 'It is the Passover sacrifice to the Lord, who passed over the houses of the Israelites in Egypt and spared our homes when he struck down the Egyptians'" (Exodus 12:26).

The Jewish people make the Passover a special holiday that nurtures in the minds of their children the memory of God's great deliverance. Jewish or not, your life is filled with holidays, special events, and moments for recognizing memorable accomplishments. A wise father uses these occasions to leave behind a trail of warm, joyful memories. Unfortunately, many of us let them pass with no awareness that they are opportunities to plant joy. They are waiting to be seized and cherished.

Our Lord teaches us by example that holidays are important and that joy can be captured within them. Find a reason to celebrate with your kids this week.

Father, teach me to revel
in the celebratory moments and
pass their joy on to children.

ALWAYS A REASON
TO CELEBRATE

God, deliver me from sullen saints.
—Teresa of Àvila

They will celebrate your abundant goodness
and joyfully sing of your righteousness.
Psalm 145:7

Need a reason to spark a celebration for your family?
Try one (or more!) of these:

- ❖ January: National Joygerm Day (8); anniversary of the first Super Bowl (12); Hat Day (19)
- ❖ February: Return Shopping Carts to the Supermarket Month; Weatherman's Day (5); anniversary of the invention of the La-Z-Boy chair (11); Northern Hemisphere Hoodie-Hoo Day (20)

❖ March: Peanut Butter Lovers' Day (1); birthday of chewing gum (19); Captain James T. Kirk's Birthday in 2228 (21); Make-Up-Your-Own-Holiday Day (26)

❖ April: The day Vel-Cro became available (2); Encourage-a-Beginning-Writer Day (10); National Honesty Day (30)

❖ May: Mother Goose Day (1); No-Socks Day (8); Visit-Your-Relatives Day (18); anniversary of the first release of *Star Wars* (25)

❖ June: National Accordion Awareness Month; Yell "Fudge" at the Cobras in North America Day (2); Hug Holiday (15); anniversary of the invention of the tennis shoe (25)

❖ July: P. T. Barnum's Birthday (5); National Ice Cream Day (21); birthday of instant coffee (25)

❖ August: National Mustard Day (5); International Left-Handers' Day (13); anniversary of the opening of the first American roller-coaster (26)

❖ September: National Chicken Month; Grandparents' Day (8); anniversary of the "Gilligan's Island" premiere (17)

❖ October: National Pizza Month; anniversary of first newspaper cartoon strip (2); anniversary of unveiling of boxer shorts (27)

❖ November: Norm Wakefield's Birthday (9); National Clean-Out-Your-Refrigerator Day (15); Mickey Mouse's Birthday (18)
❖ December: Birthday of blue jeans (5); Mike Nappa's Birthday (10); National Return-All-of-Your-Ugly-Christmas-Gifts Day (26); anniversary of the release of the bowling ball (29).

There's always a reason to celebrate; it's just a matter of finding that reason and sharing it with others. Share a celebration with your kids.

Dear Jesus, never let me forget
that having You in my life is
the best reason for celebrating!

LET'S TALK TRADITIONS

Memory feeds imagination.
—Novelist Amy Tan

And when your children ask you, "What does this ceremony mean to you?" then tell them, "It is the Passover sacrifice to the Lord. . ."
Exodus 12:26–27

How do you nurture a sense of family history? Have you developed a strategy to pass on memories that will become precious to your children? Here's how some families keep family history alive and fun.

On the first chilly night after October 31, a tradition occurs in the family of Paul and Kathy. There is hot chocolate, popcorn, and other snacks. Paul and his sons start a fire in the fireplace. When it's burning brightly, they turn out the lights and gather by the fire.

In this intimate setting, family members tell favorite

childhood memories. Mom and Dad tell of events they remember, and each child shares something from his or her past years. After several years, this has become a favorite family tradition.

Ken and Joan have children and grandchildren. On Christmas eve the whole clan comes home for a family potluck. After a meal of laughter and fun, the sharing begins. Each family member brings pictures or videos of the past year or something from several years ago. The remainder of the evening is spent reliving and sharing with other family members. If a family member is engaged to be married, the fiancé is invited to the celebration to be introduced to the family history.

When Norm and Winnie's children were young, they took 35-millimeter slides of family events. As the children grew older, they planned special evenings to review the visual family history. You'd notice lots of laughter and reminiscing as events were recalled. As the children became teenagers and young adults, they would say, "Can we look at family slides tonight?" It was an indication of how enjoyable these times had become.

Jason and Chris started a tradition before their three daughters were born. At Christmas they write a love letter to each other. They include how they've seen each other grow, how they see the Lord working through that person, and special thoughts that say "I love you." The tradition became so special they extended it to their daughters. Now each year they write a special "love letter" to each girl. They mention physical and emotional growth, a special event that occurred, and other things that seem important.

Family traditions that review family history and stimulate joyful memories of family relationships are an integral part of building a legacy of joy. Wise fathers look for ways to be deliberate and creative in reinforcing positive memories. With the fast pace of life, it becomes especially important to plant solid, positive memories as valuable building blocks for a future filled with joy.

Lord, grant that we prepare
our children's future from the
joyful building blocks of their past.

GO FLY A KITE!

Dad is destiny. More than virtually any other factor,
a biological father's presence in the family
will determine a child's success and happiness.
—*U.S. News and World Report,*
February 1995[34]

Therefore, whoever humbles himself like this child
is the greatest in the kingdom of heaven.
Matthew 18:4

Summer Saturdays were dream days for Richard and Robert. On these days the boys' father would begin tinkering with his tool kit.

First, he would buy string. Then he'd buy paper and light fuselage wood and bring it all home to the boys. Then the magic began for Richard and Robert. Fingers flying, string weaving in and out, a piece of fuselage here, a sheet of paper there.

Before long, a wonder was born: a beautiful, exciting, miraculous kite.

"Dad was a tremendous kite-maker," Robert remembered fondly. "He'd make these marvelous kites that'd fly forever. He was marvelous at it. Kids would gather around and he'd give them kites!"

The rest of the day was spent in flight. Dad would treat Richard, Robert, and other stray kids to awestruck moments of grace and laughter as their "birds" flew high in the sky. The memory of those Saturdays stuck with the boys into their adulthood, until. . .

Richard and Robert had grown up to become a team in the motion picture industry. After working long and hard on the score for a musical, the brothers were ready to write the finale, the final song and scene that would provide a happy ending and signal redemption for the misguided "villain."

It was then the joy of those summer Saturdays came to their minds. Wearing the wistful grins that come from happy reminiscing, Richard M. Sherman and Robert B. Sherman sat side-by-side at the piano and quickly penned these words:

> *With tuppence for paper and strings*
> *You can have your own set of wings*
> *With your feet on the ground you're a bird in flight*
> *With your fist holding tight to the string of your*
> *   kite. . .*

Decades after they wrote the music and lyrics to "Let's Go Fly a Kite," their father-and-sons memories have been enjoyed millions of times as the heart-satisfying ending of the Walt Disney classic, *Mary Poppins*. And it all started with a dad who was willing to share a happy day with his children.

Maybe it's time for you and your kids to go fly a kite, too.

Heavenly Father, grant me the grace
to plant a joyful memory in the hearts
of my children this Saturday.

A WALK DOWN MEMORY LANE

Our children give us the opportunity to
become the parents we always wish we had.
—Nancy Samalin[35]

Sons are a heritage from the Lord,
children a reward from him.
Psalm 127:3

"One of my earliest memories happened when I was three years old," says Mike. "I was playing with a toy—I think a Winnie the Pooh stuffed bear—and Mom called me to the front porch.

" 'Come say good-bye to your father,' she said matter-of-factly. 'He's not going to live here anymore.' My three sisters and I gathered on the porch and slowly waved farewell as Dad drove down our driveway and, for all practical purposes, out of our lives."

Mike's father moved to a small town about forty-five minutes away and continued to work near where Mike lived, but the two had only rare contact over the next dozen years. A brief holiday visit, an occasional meeting—for most of Mike's growing-up years his father was an acquaintance, like the mail carrier or the clerk at the grocery store. When Mike reached high school age, he began to think more about his lack of relationship with his father. He decided to do something about it.

"I lived a few miles from his work, so I decided that once a week or so I'd stop into his office for a visit. No agenda; just drop in and say hi. I knew his supervisors didn't mind brief family visits, so I screwed up my courage and marched in.

"Every visit was the same. He greeted me warmly, but he seemed anxious about my being there. I'd ask about his work or try to make smalltalk. He'd snap his fingers nervously, attempt a lame joke, then walk me to the door. This wasn't working. Since my grandparents lived near him, any time I visited them, I stopped by Dad's home. Again, he was cordial, but I seemed to be intruding on his plans.

"Finally, one day I sat on the army-cot bed in his one-bedroom efficiency and asked him point-blank, 'Dad, do you love me?'

"There was a pause, then he mumbled, 'Your mother says I don't know how to love.'

"'I don't care what my mother says. I just want to know if you love me.'

"He paused again, shrugged his shoulders, and said, 'I guess I don't know how to love.'

"After that, I quit trying to be part of my father's life. For the next near-decade I lived with the assumption that my father really didn't love me, his only son. Then I became a father and held my own son. I realized it's impossible not to have feelings for your own child. I decided he must love me, even if he couldn't say it.

"Recently, my father suffered a stroke that left him unable to speak. He still hasn't told me he loves me, and I guess he never will. But I can't help wondering who has lost more joy, me for not hearing it or him for passing up the simple ecstasy that comes with saying, 'I love you' to a child."

Holy Father, remind me today
to tell my children I love them.

DAD! WHEN'S MY TURN?

Two masons were asked what they were doing. The first said, "I'm putting these stones together." The second replied, "I'm building a great cathedral."
—H. Jackson Brown, Jr.[36]

Do not store up for yourselves treasures on earth, where moth and rust destroy, and where thieves break in and steal. But store up for yourselves treasures in heaven. . . . For where your treasure is, there your heart will be also.
Matthew 6:19–21

Friends of Norm's came for a visit. As they ate cookies and drank punch, Norm chatted with Rory. He asked what was memorable about Rory's childhood. This is his answer:

"I couldn't wait to get in the workshop to be with Dad and watch him build model airplanes. My muscles weren't well coordinated, but Dad would give me some small part to glue to the fuselage or wing. He'd let me choose the miniature pilot. As I grew older and steadier, I was allowed to do more.

"Dad and I would go out to the field and he would fire up the little engines. They zoomed into the air! It was so much fun to be with Dad working and flying airplanes. The day came when he gave me the controls. You can't imagine the thrill of flying the model airplane myself. Wow! To make the airplane go wherever I wanted it to go.

"Dad was good. He won flying contests. Finally Dad and I entered and won father-son events. We were a team! I grew up with this shared love for airplanes. It made me a terrible right-fielder in baseball—I was forever watching the airplanes go overhead. But that was a small price to pay.

"I joined the air force. When my tour of duty was completed, I enrolled in college and earned a degree in aviation design. I've never lost my love for airplanes—a love formed in that relationship with my dad.

"I always ask for a window seat on flights so I can watch the wing. I think of how it is constructed, how air moves over the surface, how each part does its job."

As Norm listened, he was struck again with the significance of early childhood experiences. What opportunities our Lord gives us. A father interested in airplanes shares part of his life with his son. That experience becomes a shaping memory. Rory's experience demonstrates how powerfully the bonding process shapes sons' and daughters' lives for joy or sorrow.

Newspaper columnist Wade Horn says the average teen spends thirty-five minutes a week talking with his or her father and twenty-one hours a week watching television. He reports that opinion polls indicate that parents think gifts equal love. His advice?

"Stop buying things that will eventually wear out or lose their interest. Start giving of yourself."

Dear Jesus, show me how to joyfully
give myself to my children this week.

BACK ROAD MEMORIES

I find ecstasy in living,
the mere sense of living is joy enough.
—Emily Dickinson

The joy of the Lord is your strength.
Nehemiah 8:10

C hristmas elicits all sorts of memory emotions. Norm's early experiences were filled with a giddy sense of anticipation, throttled by a father's inability to laugh and radiate joy. So Christmas season brought tension and anxiety, depending on his dad's mood.

Winnie, Norm's wife, had an entirely different experience. Norm often heard her mention going with her dad to cut down a Christmas tree. Clearly it was a fun-filled happening:

"My brother and me would go with my father to cut down the Christmas tree. This experience extended from the first grade until my high school years. In the early years we lived outside a small town in south Jersey. Dad would announce the day we were going to get a tree. If snow had fallen, we'd take our sled and traipse down a back road outside town to where trees were growing. We'd hunt until we found just the right one. Then Dad would cut it down, and we'd haul it home.

"Once the tree was set up in the house, Dad, Mom, my brother Ed, and I would have lots of fun decorating it. Dad always decorated the outside of the house, too. Even today, fifty years later, Christmas decorations mean so much to me. My dad got his joy of life from two sources. One was his love for Jesus Christ. He radiated the spirit of Christ wherever he went. He smiled, laughed, and blessed people.

"The other place he got his good humor from was his father. Every time we visited Granddad he had some new sleight-of-hand trick or gadget to surprise us. He had a sugar spoon with a hole in it so that when a person tried to get sugar it would drain out the hole. He put fake 'doggie doo' in some conspicuous place to horrify us.

"Grandpa Townsend took us for walks along the Delaware River. We stopped to skip stones across the water. He'd put a penny on the railroad track so we could see how the train wheels would flatten it. He'd tell us intriguing tales about people who lived along the river. I think his father was a riverboat captain."

The joyous spirit in her grandfather and father

infected Winnie's life. She, too, became a person who brings cheer to any situation. First she shared this spirit with her husband, who had a serious deficiency. (He once told people at a family life conference that Winnie has the ministry of mischief!) Then she taught her children how to be playful and fun loving. And her sunny disposition warms the hearts of all those who come near her.

Thanks, Grandpa Townsend and Father Wil, for passing on a heritage of joy. We all benefit from it still today.

Lord, may we remember to bless You
for giving those who
have blessed us with joy.

NEVER TOO LATE

You can't help growing older,
but you can help growing old.
—George Burns

Fathers, do not exasperate your children;
instead, bring them up in the training
and instruction of the Lord.
Ephesians 6:4

When we think of memories we often think of childhood events. Our hearts are warmed reminiscing about that special person, situation, or circumstance. But sometimes we reflect on what we wish had happened, that longed-for event that never took place. Listen as our friend Sharon tells us about one such situation.

"My dad is the best dad in the world. When I was a child I wanted to spend as much time with him as possible. Unfortunately he didn't think the way I did. He thought being a 'best dad' meant spending lots of time with his son, my brother.

"Dad fished, hunted, scouted, played, and worked with my brother. I yearned for a relationship with Dad like my brother had. I'd spend hours in the garage playing with his tools, wishing he'd show me how to use them. I'd watch him work in the yard, longing for him to show me how to create beautiful flower beds. And when he and my brother packed for a fishing trip, I wished they'd take me along.

"I grew up and got married but still carried the secret dream of spending time alone with Dad. Then five years ago an opportunity presented itself. I had the chance to open my heart to my father. To my surprise, he opened his heart to me and spoke of his regrets at not spending enough time with my sister and me.

"I said, 'Dad, I've always wished you would take me fishing with you.'

"I'll never forget his words, 'It's never too late. I'd love to take you fishing whenever you come to visit us in Idaho.'

"Now once a year I plan a long weekend with my parents. On Saturday Dad and I leave early, stop at a little mom-and-pop restaurant for breakfast, and head for the water. We bait hooks, express sincere disappointments at each other's near catches, walk the shore looking for that special spot, and share our sandwiches and cookies.

"Last September my parents celebrated their fiftieth wedding anniversary. My husband, Pat, and I traveled to Idaho to be with them. Dad and I scheduled our Saturday fishing day, but this time we took Mom and Pat along as our guests. Pat loved the experience so much that he decided to take up fishing.

"Because he's seventy-five years old and in poor health, I never know when we've fished together for the last time. But, I treasure every new opportunity and cherish the memories we've created by snatching those precious opportunities to spend time together."

Thanks, Sharon, for reminding us that we can seize the opportunity that each new day gives. Thanks for challenging us to claim now what we missed in the past.

Thank You, God,
that it's never too late.

INVESTMENT BANKERS

LOST—Somewhere between sunrise and sunset—
one golden hour, encrusted with sixty silver minutes,
each studded with sixty diamond seconds.
No reward is offered. They are lost and gone forever.
—Zig Ziglar's Little Instruction Book[37]

Jesus said, ". . .This poor widow has put more into the
treasury than all the others. They all gave out of their
wealth; but she, out of her poverty, put in everything."
Mark 12:43–44

Here's a good deal for you: For a paltry $1.5 million you, too, can own one page of Abraham Lincoln's "house divided" speech. How's that for a great investment?

Of course, if your wife prefers jewelry to history, you might consider investing instead in a thirty-three-carat Kasmir sapphire. It's a pittance at $827,000.

A 1931 movie poster of the thriller *Frankenstein* will

only put you out $198,000. For an extra $150,000 you can strum a guitar that once belonged to Elvis Presley!

Feeling adventurous? A $49,500 investment will land you a spacesuit once used by a Soviet cosmonaut. For only $5500 you can adorn yourself in a different kind of suit—armor. This finely crafted specimen is hand-hammered craftsmanship and includes an authentic sword in the glove of your metal warrior. For the more budget conscious armor-bearer, consider jousting armor at $3500. It comes complete with jousting pole.

If you prefer Asian war wear you'll definitely want to spring for the seventeenth-century Samurai armor. Made of forged metal, silks, and dyed chord, this one's a bargain at only $3400.

Too violent, you say? Aaah, how about a fiftieth-anniversary commemorative Barbie Doll for $625, a collectible Pez dispenser for $620, or the "I Love Lucy Doll" with polka dot apparel for chump change of $299.95?

You can't see yourself wasting valuable cash on any of these mightily priced products? We agree with you. We are given a certain amount of resources in life, and we must make our investments wisely. Unfortunately, we fathers are often not as careful with our time as with our money. We foolishly invest hours in overtime pay, television, Saturday business meetings, home improvement projects, the morning paper, and overconsumption of spectator sports.

Jesus "invested" His resources wisely. He didn't store up a lot of money. He made no real estate purchases. He refused to cash in on His popularity when the Jews wanted to make Him king of Israel!

Instead, our Lord deliberately chose to invest His allotment of minutes in people. He devoted years to His disciples and shared miracles with the crowds. Everything He did—including His death on the cross and subsequent resurrection—was motivated by His love for people.

Let's start making our investments of time in the people God entrusted to us. When we do that, we're halfway to the goal of leaving a legacy of happy memories.

Lord Jesus, help me to view
my time with my children
as more precious than gold.

ON BECOMING
A CHILD-MAGNET

Some of the most touching scenes in all the Bible
are those that depict Jesus with children around him.
His words about children and his actions with them
reveal his tender affection for the young.
—Roy B. Zuck (*Precious in His Sight*[38])

Let us fix our eyes on Jesus,
the author and perfecter of our faith.
Hebrews 12:2

Ever notice that some people are just natural "child-magnets?" Wherever they go, children flock to them. Jesus is one of those kinds of people. During His time on this earth, Jesus was the ultimate "child magnet." Children were drawn to Jesus. More important, Jesus was drawn to children. In every encounter, Jesus left joy in the life of a child.

Scripture records that Jesus raised three people from the dead before His crucifixion. One was His friend, Lazarus. One was a young child, and one was an adult child whose mother was in need (see Mark 5:22–43, Luke 7:11–15, and John 11:1–44).

When Jesus wanted to miraculously feed five thousand men, He used a small boy's five loaves of bread and two fish (see John 6:1–13). Talk about boosting a child's self-esteem.

Jesus repeatedly came to the defense of children, something that angered His enemies, confused His friends, and had to delight every child around. During Jesus' triumphal entry, children gathered and joyfully praised Him. The indignant Pharisees accusingly hinted that Jesus should make the children be quiet. Instead He endorsed their enthusiasm with Scripture (see Matthew 21:16). When Jesus' disciples tried to keep children from reaching Him, Jesus became angry, choosing the feelings of boys and girls over the pride of His disciples (see Matthew 19:13-15, Mark 10:13–16, and Luke 18:15–16).

Jesus was also affectionate toward children. He didn't merely shake hands with youngsters. He held them in a loving embrace (see Mark 10:16.). While He held them, Jesus spoke encouragingly to children, choosing to verbally bless them when others had cursed them (see Matthew 19:15 and Mark 10:16).

And, in an insult to adulthood, Jesus preached that children were the example of godliness (see Matthew 18:1–5, Mark 9:33–37, and Luke 9:46–48). Theologian Roy Zuck, in his enlightening book, *Precious in His Sight,* describes those moments this way:

> He [Jesus] never talked to children about what they could learn from adults, but he did tell adults some things to learn from children!
>
> How contrary to the thinking of that day, which held that adults were wise and children lacked wisdom. Since children were to learn from adults, how could adults learn from children? How shocking, then, that Jesus reversed this view!
>
> Want to enter God's kingdom? Then become like little children. Want to be great in God's eyes? Then become like little children. Want to let Jesus know you welcome and receive him? Then welcome little children.

We add: Want to be like Jesus in your own life? Then purpose to leave a legacy of joy and love for your children, just like Jesus left for you.

> *Lord, help me to joyfully love*
> *and value children as You did.*

HEAVEN IS A PLACE
WHERE JOY RESIDES

There is a ragamuffin loose on the streets of gold.
He is barefoot. He is laughing. . .and he is home.
—From a tribute to late Christian musician,
Rich Mullins

He will wipe every tear from their eyes. There will be no
more death or mourning or crying or pain,
for the old order of things has passed away.
Revelation 21:4

God is a joyful Person. In fact, He's the one who created joy in the first place, and He wants you to experience it.

A survey through the Bible reveals this to be true.
In the New International Version text of the Old and
New Testaments, the word *joy* or one of its variants (such
as joyful, rejoice, or rejoicing) is used in 373 separate

verses. That's more than one "joy verse" for each day of the year.

Scripture also reveals that the Holy Spirit is a source of joy. He filled Jesus with joy (Luke 10:21), He filled the disciples with joy (Acts 13:52), and He has the power to fill you with joy as well (Romans 15:13; Galatians 5:22).

But perhaps most telling of all is the Bible's news that heaven is a place where joy resides. Listen to this description, taken from Revelation 21:1–4, of what God has planned for us:

> Then I saw a new heaven and a new earth, for the
> first heaven and the first earth had passed
> away, and there was no longer any sea. I saw
> the Holy City, the new Jerusalem, coming
> down out of heaven from God, prepared as a
> bride beautifully dressed for her husband. And
> I heard a loud voice from the throne saying,
> "Now the dwelling of God is with men, and he
> will live with them. They will be his people,
> and God himself will be with them and be
> their God. He will wipe every tear from their
> eyes. There will be no more death or mourning
> or crying or pain, for the old order of things
> has passed away."

Can you imagine what a joyous place that will be? To live in the very presence of God? To feel His hand caress your cheek as He wipes away the tears this world has caused you? To laugh good-bye to the sorrows of death and mourning? To see the end of pain and crying? To celebrate for all eternity with the Father who loved us and sent His Son to die for us?

It makes us homesick just thinking about it. If heaven really is a place where joy resides, perhaps we should start "practicing" for heaven today by making our homes a place where joy can have a face as well—a father's face.

Holy Spirit, fill me with Your joy today
so I can make my home a
little heaven on earth for my kids.

A LITTLE CHILD
SHALL LEAD THEM

The Son alone can reveal God;
the child alone understand him.
—George MacDonald

Let the little children come to me, and do not hinder them,
for the kingdom of God belongs to such as these.
Mark 10:14

Children's hearts are soft and pliable. This truth was brought home to Norm's wife, Winnie, as she spent time with their five-year-old granddaughter, Jane.

Jane had gone to the hospital with her mother and dad to visit a young man, Brian, who was suffering from leukemia. Brian had been in the high school youth group when Jane's dad was a volunteer youth sponsor. In commenting on the hospital visit, Jane said, "He didn't look sick, but my dad said that his body was sick."

A young pastor, Neil, was also at the hospital visiting Brian and suggested that every time Jane saw a McDonald's restaurant she pray for Brian. So the day that Jane was with her grandmother, they stopped for lunch at a McDonald's. After the food had been served, Jane wanted to pray. In childlike simplicity, she prayed that the Lord would give Brian strength. Then they finished their lunch and headed home.

On the way home, they passed another McDonald's. This time Jane insisted that all four people in the car pray for Brian. "Grandma, you pray first." So Grandmother prayed for the sick man.

"Now, Aunt Annette, you pray for Brian." Annette obediently prayed. Next, Jane turned to her two-year-old brother, Ben, and instructed him that he was to pray for Brian.

"Now I'll pray," she said.

Educational psychologists tell us that teachable moments occur in the life of a child when they are especially receptive and impressionable to new truth. The incident with Jane made that point forcefully. Her parents had been involved in Brian's life when he was a teenager and were deeply touched with his physical need. No doubt Jane felt the seriousness of the situation, and her tender heart was drawn to seek the Lord's help on Brian's behalf.

Such incidents occur in our lives. Trouble is, we sometimes become desensitized to their significance. We fail to see how important both the event and our responses are to build memories of spiritual reality in the child.

And we fail to pass on that childlike faith in Jesus that should become the basis for an eternity of joy. Perhaps we should take a lesson from five-year-old Jane. Perhaps the next time you see a McDonald's, you should pray that God will help you fill the teachable moments in your children's life with the joy that comes from knowing Jesus.

Dear God, let me meet—
and greet warmly—
a teachable moment today.

PATRICK HENRY'S WILL

*There is one thing more I wish I could give
my family and that is faith in Jesus Christ.
If they had that and I had not given them
one shilling, they would be rich.*
—Patrick Henry

*Only be careful, and watch yourselves closely so that you
do not forget the things your eyes have seen or let them
slip from your heart as long as you live. Teach them to
your children and to their children after them.*
Deuteronomy 4:9

We occasionally hear a parent say, "I've started a fund for my child's college education. I know it will be expensive by the time she's ready to attend, so I'm getting a head start."

Such thoughtful planning is commendable. It's costly, but we want our children to enter into adulthood with sound job skills. It's also important to plan for your child's emotional and spiritual future.

Norm teaches a class at Phoenix Seminary on "Nurturing Your Family." It's designed to stimulate thinking about a Christian's attitude toward marriage and parenting. He asks students to list what they want their child to be like at age twenty. Six categories are suggested: physical, mental, emotional, social, spiritual, and character.

"What I've learned is that most parents don't think that way. They have an undefined desire that the child grow up to be a 'good person,' but no specific outcomes, so they have no strategy to get there. These parents want their children to have a vital relationship with Jesus Christ, but they haven't considered the hurdles to be overcome, the environment that stimulates such love, or the teaching that will lay a solid foundation.

"Winnie and I wanted our children to love the Word of God and have a habit of reading it by the time they were twenty years old. So when they were preschoolers we exposed them to books—Bible stories, fairy tales, silly poetry, and more—and created a warm, happy experience with them.

"In no time my children would toddle up to me and say, 'Read, Daddy! Read!' It was a fun, enriching experience for both parent and child—and through it the child was gaining an emotional attachment to reading and to Scripture. As they grew, we nurtured this love and the skills of reading in ways appropriate to their age. Now adults, they love the Bible and have made it an important part of their lives."

You want your child to grow up with rich, positive memories of Jesus Christ. These may be formed through Bible stories, prayer, and intimate fellowship with Him. But this outcome will not happen by chance. Building a spiritual heritage of joyful celebration is a great goal. Patrick Henry must have felt this. Listen to the words he penned in his will.

> I have now disposed of all my property to my
> family. There is one thing more I wish I could
> give them and that is faith in Jesus Christ. If
> they had that and I had not given them one
> shilling, they would be rich; and if they had not
> that, and I had given them the world, they
> would be poor indeed.

I wonder, what will you leave your children in your will? Have you planned for it?

Dear Jesus, give me a plan for passing on
my joyful relationship with You
and the courage to carry it out.

A TALE OF TWO MEN

I have never felt that football built character.
That is done by parents and church. You give us
a boy with character and we will give you back a man.
You give us a character—
and we will give him right back to you.
—Coach John McKay

The house of the righteous contains great treasure,
but the income of the wicked brings them trouble.
Proverbs 15:6

Jonathan Edwards was a godly Christian preacher. His writings reflect a deep devotion to the Lord and a passion to proclaim the gospel of Jesus Christ. Thousands have been blessed and enriched by the words he penned. But perhaps the greatest evidence of his life is seen in the heritage Edwards and his wife left behind. Of 729 descendants whose lives were traced, the marriage brought into being:

- three hundred ministers, missionaries, or theological professors;
- sixty-five college professors and fourteen presidents of colleges or universities;
- thirty judges;
- sixty authors;
- three U. S. congressmen, and one vice-president of the United States.

Max Jukes (the pseudonym used in the study to keep the real family name anonymous) lived at the same time as Edwards. He and his wife were not Christians nor people of principle. Their lives, too, bore fruit as the record of 1026 descendants tells. There were at least:

- 310 vagrants and 100 alcoholics;
- seven murderers;
- 110 who went to prison for an average of thirteen years each;
- 200 public prostitutes, and
- sixty habitual thieves.

It's been estimated that the Jukes descendants cost the government over $1 million. More costly has been the heartbreak and grief the Jukes clan brought on thousands of people's lives—their own included. It would be hard to estimate the damage to human life this family has caused.

Many years ago Norm came across a quotation of unknown origin. He made it into a plaque that now hangs in his office. The quotation reads: "A teacher affects eternity. You can never tell where his influence stops." Norm has spent his life in various forms of teaching, mentoring, or encouraging others in their Christian faith, so those words have motivated and challenged him to invest his life wisely.

Like Edwards and Jukes, every father is a teacher. Every man has the opportunity to invest his life in those values that endure. The examples of the Edwards and Jukes lineages are graphic, but all of us leave behind a heritage of good or evil, of kindness or selfishness, of love or hate, happiness or sorrow.

Which will you leave?

Lord Jesus, let my life be a blessing
to my children, not a curse.

THE MARK

Early Christians were filled with joy because Jesus
gave them hope and life. Should we be any different?
—*The Minister's Little Devotional Book*[39]

And he took the children in his arms,
put his hands on them and blessed them.
Mark 10:16

The beat-up old Harley-Davidson motorcycle wasn't even for sale when Bob saw it in the corner of the garage. But this was a garage sale, after all. It wouldn't hurt to ask.

"Is the bike for sale?"

After scratching his chin in thought, the owner decided he might as well sell it. "But I'll warn ya," he said, "that bike hasn't run since I've had it. Motor's seized up."

Bob was a fair mechanic, and he figured with a little fixing up, he could make a few bucks. Bob and the owner agreed on a scrap-yard price of $35. The next day Bob hauled it off to his garage, where it sat.

Bob finally checked over the bike and made a list of the major parts he'd need. Then he called Harley-Davidson to check the costs. That's when things got a little strange.

The customer service representative asked for the serial number on the Harley to track down the right parts. He put Bob on hold. Bob waited. . .and waited. . .and waited. He was about to hang up when the parts agent came back on the line: "I'm going to have to call you back, okay?" He sounded nervous. "Could I get your full name, address, and phone number, please?" It seemed an unusually detailed request for part prices, but Bob gave it and hung up, shaking his head.

Days passed without any word. Then the phone rang, only it wasn't the parts guy, but an executive with the Harley-Davidson company. "Listen, Bob," the executive said carefully, "I want you to do something for me: Take the seat off your bike and see if anything is written underneath."

Muttering the whole way, Bob followed the man's instructions. When he unscrewed the seat and turned it over, he found it was engraved with these words: "THE KING." Then Bob discovered that the scrap-yard-bound motorcycle had been owned by the late Elvis Presley. Harley-Davidson immediately offered him $300,000 for the bike. A few days later, entertainer Jay Leno called and personally offered $500,000. Suddenly, Bob was going to make a half-million dollars on a $35 investment, simply because Elvis had left his mark under the seat.[40]

That now-famous Harley is a nice bike, but there's nothing all that special about it. It's been outclassed a dozen times over since Elvis rode around on it. But the fact that it had been "touched" by the king of rock-n-roll made it worth a fortune.

Your children are cute, to be sure, but nothing looks unusually special about them. Your mark as their father is hidden beneath the surface. Years from now, will that mark reveal a legacy of joy? If so, you'll have given them value far beyond any of Elvis's toys.

King Jesus, touch my life
with Your joy, so I may leave
that mark on my children's lives.

I WILL MAKE YOU
FISHERS OF A BOY

*The difference between catching men and catching fish is
that you catch fish that are alive, and they die;
you catch men that are dead and bring them to life.*
—Dawson Trotman

*A friend loves at all times,
and a brother is born for adversity.*
Proverbs 17:17

The men had come to the retreat center to encourage each other to live significant lives. Each confessed a relationship with Jesus Christ and felt challenged to be a better husband, father, or friend. In this context Art shared his story:

"Dad was gone from the home early in my memories. Mom loved us and worked hard to provide for our needs, but she couldn't be both a mother and a father.

Somewhere during grade school I developed a strong interest in fishing. I read fishing magazines. I'd go to K-Mart and look through their fishing equipment. I bought a rod and reel. The only problem was I had no one to take me fishing. None of the friends I knew fished.

"Then one day someone told me that a couple of retired men at church were avid fishermen. I began to hang around them, listening to their fishing exploits, dropping hints that I'd like to go with them.

" 'Oh, we might take you sometime,' Charlie said, but nothing happened. Then one day I came home from school, and Mom announced, 'Charlie called and invited you to go fishing with him and Bill tomorrow morning. You'll have to be ready early. They'll stop by for you shortly before six.'

"Wow, was I excited! I didn't think I could sleep that night. I was up at the crack of dawn, waiting for them. I must have been an odd sight to these veteran anglers. It didn't take long before they were saying, 'Now, son, let me show you how to cast properly.' . . . 'This is the way you tie a hook on the line.'

"So these two old-timers let a young boy join their fishing. I can't tell you what it meant. Not only did my love for fishing become a reality, but I'll always prize their friendship.

"About a year ago I was reflecting on the priceless

heritage these men had given me. Then I thought of two young brothers in my church that didn't have a dad. I asked them if they'd like to go fishing with me. You ought to have seen their faces light up!

"So we went fishing. Their lines were zinging dangerously close to my head, so I said, 'Now, boys, let me show you how to cast properly.' . . . 'This is the way you tie a hook on the line.'"

Somewhere a child waits to be invited into a man's life. To share some mutual interest; to go to a sports event; to build memories; to laugh together; to say, "You're significant." Is that child at your church or in your neighborhood—or perhaps living in your home?

Father, I offer myself anew to You today.
Use me to bring joy to children around me.

WHAT'S IN A NAME?

Our children are our greatest legacy.
They are our most valuable investment.
There is no better hope, no surer joy,
and no finer accomplishment than having set
the next generation up the narrow road.
—George Grant and Karen Grant[41]

I rejoiced with those who said to me,
"Let us go to the house of the Lord."
Psalm 122:1

Some church names have an entertaining quality about them. We've seen storefront churches with names so long it sounded like their statement of faith. We heard of a church near Chicago's O'Hare airport that is called "The King James Bible Baptist Church."

At one church considering a name change, for which the original initials were LPBC, members submitted some interesting suggestions:

- ❖ Ideal Bible Church
- ❖ Lasting Peace Bible Church
- ❖ Let's Party Bible Church
- ❖ Lots of Potluck Bible Church
- ❖ New and Improved Assembly of Hope
- ❖ Non-denominational Evangelical Premillennial Bible Church
- ❖ Sunnyside Community Church Fellowship Assembly Bible Chapel
- ❖ Newest Hope Bible Chapel
- ❖ Lord's People Bible Chapel

Fortunately none of those were accepted. But sometimes church names do send a strange message to outsiders. A church in No Hope, Kentucky, for example, calls itself "No Hope Christian Church."

More important than the name is what goes on inside the congregation. What do our children experience at "church?" Are they building positive memories? We recall a child telling his parent, "My teacher made me sit still so I couldn't learn anything!" Tragically some children dread going to church because it's dull and boring. For them church is something they have to do, not something they get to do.

Norm is involved in a children's ministry called "Grace Place" at his church. The program uses skits and drama and fun, creative learning. Team members want children to grow up with lots of positive memories from going to church. Each child who leaves chooses whether to give a hug or a "high five." Team members frequently tell the children how much God loves them and show their own love as well.

A parent will report, "Shawn looks forward to going to Grace Place. He can't wait to get there." Such reports mean the children are accumulating joyful memories of being with the Lord's people, learning of Christ's love, and strengthening their trust in their heavenly Father.

Christ never meant the church to be a dreary, dull affair for children. What can you do to give your child joyful memories of the house of God?

Lord Jesus, thank You for the joy
to be found in a local church.
Please help me and my family
contribute to that joy this week.

EVEN JOY GETS
A FEW BLISTERS!

*Cheerfulness is the great lubricant of the wheels
of life. It lightens labor, diminishes difficulties,
and mitigates misfortunes.*
—*Strength for a Man's Heart*[42]

Be joyful always.
1 Thessalonians 5:16

Paul and Silas, leaders of the Christian church in the first century, were determined to spread joy regardless of circumstance. After a false accusation, these men were arrested and brought before a hostile crowd. Without a trial, both men were stripped, severely beaten, and chained in a dark prison cell.

In that situation you probably would have been both angry and discouraged. You might have felt like cursing your jailers or plotting revenge on enemies who had unjustly robbed you of your freedom and bodily abused you.

But no experience and no person, however cruel, could take the joy from Paul and Silas. Regardless of the horrible, abusive things people did to them, they were still loved by God. So they sang. Two bloody, falsely accused prisoners who should have been groaning in their chains were singing hymns of joy for their cellmates and jailers (Acts 16:16–40).

If only we could have that determination to spread joy in the face of disaster. If only we could refuse to give up when life tries to beat down our families. If only we could. . .

But with God's help, we can.

Here's a saying worth remembering:

Every man is enthusiastic at times. One man has enthusiasm for thirty minutes, another has it for thirty days—but it is the man that has it for thirty years who makes a success in life.

Your children don't need a legacy of fizzled-out delight. They need a father who is enthusiastic about planting joy for thirty years and beyond.

It's difficult to create happy memories for your family. Financial circumstances pressure everyone. That adoring preschooler turns into a sarcastic teenager. A joyful expression feels like a facade masking discouragement.

God has forgotten to answer your prayers. Your child suffers from debilitating illness. Your daughter abuses drugs. Your son dates a girl whose values are opposite yours. . . .

During times like these, determination to spread joy into your family must overcome feelings of surrender. Darkness in life is no excuse for abandoning joy. In fact, C. S. Lewis in *Letters to an American Lady* declared that, just as shadows make up half the beauty of the world, "shadows" in life can accent the beauty we find in it.

Perhaps it's time we started finding the beauty in shadows for our families.

> *Creator God, teach me to see*
> *the beautiful things that are obscured*
> *in life's deep shadows.*

RISKY BUSINESS

Jesus left few traces of himself on earth. He wrote no
books or even pamphlets. A wanderer, he left no home or
even belongings that could be enshrined in a museum.
He did not marry, settle down, and begin a dynasty.
We would, in fact, know nothing about him except for
the traces he left in human beings. That was his design.
—Philip Yancey (*The Jesus I Never Knew*[43])

Watch out that you do not lose what you have worked for,
but that you may be rewarded fully.
2 John 8

As a male, you are ten times more likely to die from
falling into a hole than is your wife—or any other
female. In fact, your life is fraught with risk.

Larry Lauden decided to find out exactly how much
risk is involved in our typical American lives. He shared
his statistical findings in *The Book of Risks*[44]. Here are a

few things he discovered:

Just being a man is a high-risk endeavor. The male death rate is substantially higher than that for females at every life period from birth until old age.

Men are two times more likely to die from excessive cold, car accidents, accidental poisoning, lung cancer, tuberculosis, heart disease, and dog bites. They're three times as likely to die from suffocation, alcoholism, homicide, and accidents in general. Lightning is four times more likely to strike a man. Airplane crashes are six times more likely to kill a man. Police gunfire is thirty-two times more likely to kill a man. In war, sixty men die for each woman casualty.

Living in America is risky, too. One-third of all Americans are injured each year. A tornado touches down in the U.S. on the average of two times a day, with one in 100 tornadoes killing someone. One in 500 Americans dies of cancer each year.

Then there are man-made disasters. If we were in a gathering of 1000, an average 242 of us would have been in a traffic accident in the past year, 200 would have had our homes burgled, seventy-two of us would have been theft victims, thirty-one of us would have been victims of violent crime, and one poor soul among us would be dead—murdered.

But don't worry about being blown up in a U.S. terrorist bombing. Only one in three million are. Your chances of receiving a live letter bomb in the next year are one in fifteen million. And, your risk of being struck and killed by a meteor is about one in five billion.

Jesus lived a risky life. Knowing He had a certain number of years on earth, He decided to spend them on people, to risk the entire future on eleven men who would abandon Him in His hour of greatest need.

Many would call that risk too great, but Jesus could see into today, into the eyes of Mike, Norm, and you who would be part of His kingdom as a result of those disciples' work. In the end, the greatest risk for Christ would have been not to risk at all.

As a father, the "risk factor" multiplies with each child you call your own. Together with your children, you face an uncertain future. Our advice? Reduce the risk of an unhappy future by following Jesus' example of risk management. Invest your life in people—your children.

Jesus, show me how to safely risk
planting joy in my kids' childhood.

FED-UP FAMILY MEMBERS

Handle this child carefully. Remember,
you're dealing with a sensitive, high-strung little stinker.
—Child specialist to new mother

Train a child in the way he should go,
and when he is old he will not turn from it.
Proverbs 22:6

Tom Hansen was fed up. He'd had enough. It was pay-back time.

So Tom filed suit in a Colorado District Court in April 1978. He sued his parents for $350,000 in damages.

His complaint? They were bad parents who had wrecked his life.

Tom contended that their willful and wanton neglect had left him with deep-rooted problems that would require psychiatric attention for the rest of his life. His lawyer said, "Basically what we are doing is bringing a suit for malpractice of parenting."

So he sued his parents for $250,000 in medical costs and $100,000 in punitive damages.

But wait. There's also a flip side to this scenario of fed-up family members. Anyone for a parent's view?

In 1982 Anne Bullington went on strike against her family. Anne sat outside her house in a lawn chair for six days with protest signs that read, "Mother on Strike" and "Have You Hugged Your Mother Today?" She struck until her five children agreed to her demands.

She felt her children needed to realize that she was a human being and deserved a little affection and consideration. "Children forget that a mother has her own life. They forget to talk to me. They forget to kiss me. They didn't think of me as a person. They thought of me as a mother—someone who owed them something."

Whatever the outcomes of Tom Hansen's malpractice suit and Anne Bullington's picketing actions have been, we are certain that they have affected happiness and the spirit of life in those two families in some ways. Now many years later, do the Bullingtons look back on these events with laughter and thankfulnes? Or are there memories that still generate feelings of resentment, bitterness, and anger?

Thousands of years ago, the godly man Joshua was able to speak for himself and his family when he said, "As for me and my house we will serve the Lord" (Joshua 24:15).

His words express a unity of spirit within his family. They could move forward together in the events of life without resentment and bitterness.

The genuineness of a parent's faith must have penetrated Joshua's children's lives, creating an environment of unity.

Let us be men who do likewise.

Father, use me today to generate joy,
not bitterness, in the spirit of my family.

LEGACY LOST AND FOUND

*As fathers, our actions today are writing the future of
America—not with ink and paper, but with flesh and
blood, through our active involvement
in the lives of our children.*
—Ken Canfield, Ph.D.[45]

*Fathers, do not embitter your children,
or they will become discouraged.*
Colossians 3:21

Eleven tough years Gary Rosberg had worked toward earning his doctoral degree in counseling, and now the dream was a few weeks from realization. The final hurdle, his doctoral thesis, was nearing completion. After that, graduation!

Gary sat in his office, buried in a pile of research for that thesis, when his mental effort was momentarily interrupted. His young daughter, Sarah, bounced in to show off a picture she had drawn. She called it her "Rosberg Family Portrait." Deep in concentration, at first Gary didn't notice. Then he paused long enough to say a few encouraging words to his young artist.

When Sarah left the room, Gary looked at the picture once more. Something was wrong, and he couldn't yet put his finger on it. Then it hit him. Daddy was missing from the collection of stick figures on the page. Mom was there, Sarah was there, sister Missy was there, even the family dog was there. But no Dad.

Gary called Sarah back, pointed to the picture, and asked, "Honey, where's your daddy?"

"You're at the library," Sarah explained matter-of-factly. Then she went back out to play.

Over the next weeks, Gary thought about what the past eleven years had cost. When he asked his wife, Barbara, she replied, "The girls and I love you very much. We want you home. But you haven't been here. I've felt like a single parent for years."

Gary knew she was right. He remembered vacations canceled so he could attend classes, dinners he'd skipped to study, a time Missy refused to sit on his lap because she didn't know her daddy.

At that point, Gary Rosberg decided it was time to come home. Seeking a group of men to hold him accountable, Gary began the long, arduous process of "winning" back his family. He made his family a top priority, scheduling time around them. He devoted himself to attending the girls' basketball games, to picking up pizza, and to spending time alone with his wife. Thankfully, his family welcomed him with open arms.

"I almost blew my legacy," Gary says. "I had blocked my family out. Nothing could get through. It took the naiveté of a little girl to break through the wall that eleven years of college and a full-time job had built around my heart."

Gary's renewed efforts at building his legacy are paying off. Not long ago, Sarah painted a new family portrait. This time, stick-figure Dad was right in the middle of the clan. "That picture stays on the wall of my office so I can always see it," Gary says.

Gary reflects, "What God is telling us men is that we can go back home and leave a healthy legacy. Believe me, if I can come back home, so can you."[46]

> *Lord, turn my heart toward home*
> *so I can leave a legacy of being involved*
> *in the lives of my children.*

HANDS-ON FATHERING

Dads make a difference.
—John Trent

And if anyone gives even a cup of cold water to one of
these little ones because he is my disciple, I tell you the
truth, he will certainly not lose his reward.
Matthew 10:42

Joyful fathering should be a hands-on business, and when it is, there's no limit to what kinds of rewards it'll bring. Just ask Michael Haas and his son Chris.

A former high school coach, Michael harbors a love for the game of basketball. It's no surprise, then, that Michael shared that love with Chris, teaching him how to play from toddlerhood. By the time Chris was only thirteen, those hours of father-son games already were paying off big time.

When Chris was nine years old, he enjoyed playing a good pick-up game with other kids at his grade school.

But they always seemed to make fundamental mistakes in shooting. "I thought I could help them by putting hands on the ball to show the proper way to shoot."

Encouraged by his dad, Chris went home and stuck his hands in poster paint. He slapped those wet-paint hands onto a basketball, leaving handprints that indicated just the right spots for holding a ball to maximize shooting accuracy.

It worked. Four years later, Chris's Hands-on Basketball was a national product in stores. It was turning about a $50,000 profit a year for Chris. Soon there was Hands-on Football, a junior-sized football with handprints showing the best grip for passing.

Although the lines are all Chris's ideas, he's quick to point out that his dad had a "hand" in the development of these products—and a hand in their inspiration.[47]

British athlete Derek Redmond got a different kind of hand from his father. Redmond was expected to medal at the 1992 Barcelona Summer Olympics. A gold medal in the 400-meter race was possible.

During the semifinal heat, Derek was putting his world-class speed on display when the unthinkable happened. He suddenly felt a searing pain in the back of his leg. Falling crippled to the track, he realized he had torn his hamstring. In agony, both physical and emotional, he watched the other runners race past him.

But when the medical crew came jogging out, Derek

waved them off and hobbled to his feet. He would finish the race, no matter what. Pathetically courageous, he began hopping down the track. Unexpectedly, a determined man bounded out of the grandstands, pushed past a security guard, and raced onto the track beside Derek. It was Derek's father, Jim Redmond.

Derek put his arm over his dad's shoulders, and with his father supporting his weight, the two of them painfully made their way to the finish line, careful to stay in Derek's lane the whole way. When they crossed, applause thundered throughout the stadium. Father and son received a standing ovation from everyone.

Sports Illustrated commented, "Derek Redmond didn't walk away with the gold medal, but he walked away with an incredible memory of a father who, when he saw his son in pain, left his seat in the stands to help him finish the race."[48]

Hands-on fatherhood yields untold rewards, not the least of which are joyful memories for our children. Our involvement in their daily lives is irreplaceable.

Dear God, this week
show me how to be involved with
my children in hands-on ways.

OPPORTUNITIES TO ENCOURAGE

No one is useless in this world who
lightens the burden of it to anyone else.
—Charles Dickens

Pleasant words are a honeycomb,
sweet to the soul and healing to the bones.
Proverbs 16:24

What do you do when your child makes a mistake? Or fails? Our reactions to crises leave a trail of memories that can bless or haunt our children. Internal tapes replay the consequences of the past. What those tapes play in our heads from years past can immobilize us with shame.

Bill is a robust, bright man in his fifties. He has a genuine love for Jesus and for people. Yet Bill is plagued by memories of perceived failure. His face is etched with marks of anxiety and pain. He is hypersensitive to what others think of him.

When he was a young boy nothing Bill did brought praise and affirmation from his severe, exacting father. However hard he tried, it was never enough. It was as though he were climbing a ladder to reach acceptance. One day he realized that the ladder never ended. He never would be loved and cherished. What a crushing blow!

Children need our support when they fail. Sometimes we understand and give it; sometimes we don't see from a loving perspective and we blow it. Norm hasn't forgotten when Jody had received that long-awaited driver's license. She asked if she could drive the family car to school.

"I had a little apprehension because she was so new in this skill, but I said, 'Yes, you can do it.' She had been gone about fifteen minutes and I was washing dishes in the kitchen. As I stood at the sink, I saw Jody suddenly pull into the carport. The front of our car was smashed in. What a shock!

"In the thirty seconds before my daughter entered the house, my mind did some lightning data processing. I had just enough time to realize that Jody was more important than my car. So when this heartbroken, teary-eyed teenager dragged into the house, I put my arms around her, hugged her warmly, and asked, 'Are you okay?'

" 'Yes, but the car's smashed up,' she sobbed.

" 'The car can be repaired,' I said. 'What's important to me is that you're not injured.'

"When Jody told her friends they were amazed. 'You

mean he didn't yell at you? My dad would have killed me if I'd done something like that.'

"On another day I might have reacted that way, but I'm grateful that in this particular time of crisis Jody could feel protected and cherished. The car did get repaired, and the accident is a faded memory. We look back on 'the wreck incident' with chuckles and positive feelings.

"I'm glad that I chose the right response. Jody was (and is still) more important to me than the car. We no longer have the car, but she continues to bring joy to my heart."

Holy Spirit, guide me daily
to make joyful responses to
potentially tragic situations.

HOW TO BE AN
INFECTIOUS PERSON

Parents cannot change the color of their child's eyes,
but they can give to eyes the light
of understanding's warmth of sympathy.
—Charles Kingsley[49]

He is like a tree planted by streams of water,
which yields its fruit in season and whose leaf
does not wither. Whatever he does prospers.
Psalm 1:3

Chances are you've never heard of Mary Mallon. She was an infectious person who influenced many people as a cook in New York City. In 1907 officials from the City Department of Health discovered that she was a carrier of typhoid fever bacteria though she had a resistance to contracting the dreaded disease herself. She became known as "Typhoid Mary."

For three years doctors treated Mary. She signed a commitment not to work as a cook. She reported quarterly to the Health Department. Then Mary dropped out of sight.

In 1915 typhoid again erupted among food handlers at a city hospital. The culprit was "Typhoid Mary." Authorities decided the only way to control Mary's infectious influence was to institutionalize her. She was quarantined until her death in 1938.

Typhoid Mary gained notoriety for infecting others with a deadly disease. Many fathers are remembered because they leave a trail of emotionally and spiritually diseased lives. They infect their children with bitterness, sensuality, greed, or sarcasm. The infection is inside; we only see the outward manifestations of destructive behavior.

Even people from biblical history adversely infected their children. The Old Testament patriarch, Abraham, for example, passed on a weakness for deceit to his son, Isaac. Abraham moved to Gerar with his beautiful wife, Sarah. Abraham feared that the king would kill him to make Sarah an available widow. So Abraham said, "She is my sister." Sure enough, the king added Sarah to his family. The Lord had to intervene to save the day (Genesis 20).

When Abraham's son, Isaac, faced an identical situation many years later, he employed the same tactic. He, too, passed off his wife, Rebekah, as his sister (Genesis 26). The father's disease had successfully infected the son. Then

Isaac and Rebekah had a son, Jacob. He is famous for his skillful use of deceit to gain what he wanted, even using it to rob his brother.

When Jacob became an adult and had a family, his own sons practiced deceit toward him, lying to him about the death of their brother, Joseph. The truth was they'd sold Joseph into slavery (Genesis 37). Four generations of infectious influence brought about much suffering.

We infect the next generation for good or ill. Our interactions with them sow the seeds that bear the fruit of joy and prosperity or bitterness and barrenness. The Bible warns us that "God cannot be mocked. A man reaps what he sows" (Galatians 6:7). In no other circumstance is this more true than among our children.

Dear Lord, thank You for making joy contagious.
Help me to infect my children today.

TOOTHPASTE
FOR CHRISTMAS

I have nothing to offer but blood, toil, tears, and sweat.
—Winston Churchill

Each man should give what he has decided
in his heart to give, not reluctantly or under
compulsion, for God loves a cheerful giver.
2 Corinthians 9:7

Mary Kay Beard laughed with derision at the "gifts" the church group brought for her and the other prisoners that Christmas. Toothpaste and soap weren't her ideas of holiday presents. Still, she noticed that other inmates at the women's detention center were glad to get them, carefully hoarding and trading them among themselves.

A few months earlier Mary Kay had been sitting at rock bottom in a solitary confinement cell. There she started reading the Bible and had become a Christian. Now back in general population, the convict stopped to notice the other women.

As Christmas neared, she noticed inmates wrap the miniature tubes of toothpaste and bars of soap they'd received from the church. On "family day"—Christmas— the incarcerated mothers lovingly presented their humble gifts to their children.

"Most children wouldn't think much of such small gifts," Mary Kay says, "but in prison there was such joy on their faces! It didn't really matter to them what they got; it was from *Mama*."

Mary Kay realized that what these mothers most wanted to give their kids was a little bit of joy before saying good-bye and returning to their cells. In 1976 Mary Kay was released from prison, but the memories of those children gleefully tearing open toothpaste presents stuck with her. Just over five years later, while working with the international Prison Fellowship Ministries organization in Alabama, she had an idea: What if people on the outside would buy Christmas presents for children of inmates? Enlisting the support of other Prison Fellowship volunteers and a local mall, they made arrangements to set up Christmas trees with children's names on paper ornaments shaped like angels. Shoppers were encouraged to buy an extra gift for a child whose father or mother was in prison.

Project Angel Tree was born. The first "angel trees"

went up the day after Thanksgiving in 1982. Mary Kay hoped the project would bring joy to 200 or so children that Christmas. Instead, 556 kids received gifts. On a Christmas many years later, Project Angel Tree brought smiles to about 500,000 children. But Mary Kay knows they're not just giving presents through her little idea. They're giving moments of joy to America's young.[50]

The ability to give joy to a child is a precious gift, something thousands of parents in prison can't do easily. Yet God has probably given you the opportunities each day, or frequently, if you cannot live with your children. What will you do with your precious gift?

Dear God, make me like You—
a giver of joy each day of the year.

CHRISTMAS FRIENDS

Long after I'm gone, what I did today will be heard by
someone. I just want them to get the best of what I had.
—Elvis Presley

The Lord Jesus himself said:
"It is more blessed to give than to receive."
Acts 20:35

The message on the answering machine was strange. In an obviously disguised voice, someone hissed, "We're your Christmas Friends. Check your front door!"

A holiday prank? A crank caller? Uncertain of what he'd find, Mike went to the front door. Hanging from the doorknob was a gaily decorated stocking filled with small gifts and a note that began:

'Twas the first night of Christmas when all
through your house

Not a creature was stirring except a mouse.
Then suddenly, several little souls did appear
It's your Christmas friends to bring your holiday
    cheer!

The rest of the note informed Mike and his family that each night until Christmas they were to re-hang the stocking on the front door for the "Christmas Friends" to fill. No peeking allowed.

So began the twelve days leading up to Christmas at the Nappas'. Five-year-old Tony could barely contain his excitement each night. What new trinket or fun surprise would his Christmas Friends leave in the stocking? On Christmas Eve the friends revealed their identity by singing carols on the porch as they left their last Christmas gift. Tony will never forget the joy of that Christmas.

When the next Christmas rolled around, Tony was even more excited than usual. It wasn't that he'd be getting more Christmas Friends. He didn't. That year he was going to *be* a Christmas Friend.

The light of joy of the previous year was a dim candle compared to the fire of joyful giving that burned in Tony. He bounded up and down the aisles to find just the right toys, just the right candies, just the right things to give to the family he'd picked out. With extra care, he chose just the right stocking to bear those gifts.

Each evening he could barely contain himself until it was time to brave the ice and snow to deliver that night's "load" to the chosen family. Each night he giggled with breathless delight, sneaking up to the door, depositing his bounty, and racing away into the dark. To be sure, everything he put in the stocking was something he wanted himself, but for Tony the sheer joy of giving outweighed the delight of receiving. He was hooked.

Years later, Tony talks with joy about that Christmas he was an "undercover elf." And each year he plans some new way to secretly give something to others.

Tony's childlike spirit reminds us as fathers that one of the greatest joys in life is found in giving to others. Let's be fathers who teach our children by example to be generous givers, so they can discover that joy for themselves.

Lord, we praise You for making the art
of giving such a joyous thing!

CLEAN YOUR MESSES!

Waitress to customer: "Have a nice day!"
Customer to waitress: "I'm sorry,
but I've made other plans!"[51]

This is a day you are to commemorate;
for the generations to come you shall celebrate it
as a festival to the Lord—a lasting ordinance.
Exodus 12:14

For many years Norm has kept a highly classified personal file that he guards jealously. It's his collection of cherished memories that others have shared with him.

Mostly this top-secret dossier consists of encouraging cards and letters that he has received. Occasionally other scraps of memorabilia find their way into this sacred place because they are simply too touching to lose.

One four-inch-by-eight-inch sheet of notebook paper is in the latter category. It stirs up particular warmth:

"I had been invited to speak at a men's conference in Boise, Idaho. The meeting had been planned by Dennis Mansfield, a good friend, so I looked forward to spending time with the Mansfields as well as speaking. For the one night I would be in town, he and his wife, Susan, invited me to stay at their home so we would have an opportunity to talk together.

"Their home had limited space, but their daughter, Megan, volunteered to give up the use of her room for the night so that I might have a comfortable place to rest.

"That evening as I was getting ready for bed, I noticed a small piece of notebook paper with my name on it lying in a prominent spot. Here was the message written to me:

I hope you like my room. Plees make the
beds and cleen up your messes!

Megan.

"My first reaction was to laugh at this honest word of instruction. Then I found myself touched with tenderness for Megan and her childlike spirit of forthrightness. The message was so meaningful, I knew I'd have to keep it in a safe place."

Norm learned something important from this little girl who was willing to share her room but wanted it to be cared for. He realized that cherished memories are among the best building blocks for positive relationships. They enrich our relationships with children and give them special meaning. Though several years have passed, Megan and the memories of that night as a guest in her home linger in Norm's heart.

Parents and other significant adults may allow delightful memories to fade and pass away unless they periodically pause to reminisce over them. It probably won't matter if you can't remember the major exports of Tanzania or the pronunciation of the Russian alphabet. But those endearing incidents with your children that happened yesterday or a year ago have the power to bring a smile to your face and warmth to your heart.

Take time to revel in your own special memories today.

Lord, help me gather and hold
in my mind the unique blessings
You have given to me through my kids.

COUNSEL FROM KIDS

When the clever are really intelligent,
they look to children for answers.
—Diane M. Komp, M.D.[52]

And he said: "I tell you the truth,
unless you change and become
like little children, you will never
enter the kingdom of heaven."
Matthew 18:3

In preparation for this book, Norm rummaged through files of notes, illustrations, and remembrances. He came across a collection of letters, cards, and notes his children had written to their parents, part of the heritage of joy in the Wakefield clan.

Jill wrote this brief response to a note Norm had sent to her:

Dear Dad, Thank you for your note. I really appreciated it. I was down today. Then I read it. Just at the right time and day. I pray for you a lot. Smell the paper. It smells like peaches. Yum. I love you loads and loads and loads. I really do.

Your daughter, Jill

Years ago on Mothers' Day, daughter Jody wrote the following on a card:

"Love: n. 1. a deep devotion or affection for a person or persons."

That's what the dictionary says, but I don't agree. Sure, that's part of love, but they left out the important parts. Parts like understanding. Listening. Smiling. Laughing. And hugging.

And, boy, did they leave out patience! There are also a lot of other things I could add; things that are hard to describe in words. So, I guess I won't try to, because I've seen what love is,

I've seen you, Mom.

Norm was having physical problems when he received a note from his daughter, Amy.

ADVICE FROM DAD TO DAUGHTER: Cars need regular attention—check oil and other fluids, belts and tires at least once a month. It's cheaper to take care of the car you have than to buy a new one.

ADVICE FROM DAUGHTER TO DAD: Bodies need regular attention—check oil and other fluids, belts and tires at least once every three years. I can get a new car, but I can't get a new dad.

Is it time for you to see the mechanic?

I love you! Amy

Healthy family relationships are reciprocal. Parents view their children as gifts from a loving Father and prize and delight in them. They love, affirm, enjoy, and nurture them. What we sometimes forget is that our children are also investing in us.

When they're little they snuggle in our lap and smile at us in ways that melt our hearts. As they grow up they bless us in other endearing ways. Adults who don't recognize these acts of love and don't collect and cherish them are the poorer. Their loss is felt by both parent and child.

Allowing our children to nurture memories in us energizes us and gives us a healthy perspective on family relationships.

Dear God, thank You for making me a father.

MEMORIES IN WOOD

*One of my most important accomplishments is to
be a huge success in the grandparenting business.*
—former U.S. President George Bush

*Every good and perfect gift is from above,
coming down from the Father of the heavenly lights.*
James 1:17

B ill Thrall is a pastor at Norm's church. He is held
in high esteem inside and outside the church family
for his love for Christ and his unique gifts for helping
individuals find healing from life's hurts. It was through
Bill's example that Norm was challenged to think about a
father's legacy.

When they were first acquainted, Bill invited Norm to
see some products of his woodworking hobby. Bill explained
that each year he undertakes a major woodworking project as a Christmas present for someone in his family. The

craftsmanship in the fine pieces of furniture he makes seem wondrous. Bill made a china cabinet for his daughter. She found the style she wanted in a magazine. Bill took the picture and drew a design. He reproduced the precise angles and curves, made the intricate maneuvers for pedestals, knobs, and swirls. The finished cabinet shows the quality and skill of a true craftsman.

Bill puts more into the work than his talent. Each step of the designing, cutting, sanding, gluing, and finishing are invested with his love for his wife and children.

What really captured my attention was what Bill is accomplishing for his children and grandchildren. With his joy-filled labors, he's leaving behind a heritage of happy memories that can be seen, handled, sat in, leaned on, and appreciated for generations.

Twenty-five or thirty years into the future, we envision Bill's grandchildren telling their children about this great man who lovingly labored to leave behind a remembrance of his devotion to his family. We can see a great-grandchild carefully placing her china in the treasured cabinet that's been passed on to her, wishing she could have known its maker.

Bill's personal love and warm relationships with children and grandchildren match his woodworking skill. On our Friday morning walks, Norm's friend shares with delight the adventures he's had with his grandchildren. He laughs as he describes his fishing expeditions or humorous moments at home. The mutual joy shared by granddad and grandchild will leave powerful and rich memories.

Moses stood before the burning bush at the Lord's commissioning service. The lowly shepherd felt inadequate to fulfill God's mission. However, the Lord showed him that he could use a stick in his hand to perform miracles— if he would use it.

We may not have Bill's skill for woodworking, but our Lord has placed some special ability in the hands of every father. We, like Bill, need to learn how to use our individual talents to fashion special memories for our children and grandchildren.

Father, help me to use the "stick" You've
placed in my hand to leave a lasting,
happy memory for my
children and grandchildren.

MULTIPLICATION TABLES

"Psst. . .Susie! What's 12 + 7?"
"A BILLION."
"Thanks! Wait a minute. That can't be right. . .
That's what she said 3 + 4 was."
—"Calvin and Hobbes" cartoon by Bill Watterson

Still other seed fell on good soil. It came up,
grew and produced a crop, multiplying thirty,
sixty, or even a hundred times.
Mark 4:8

Multiplication is an interesting concept. You start with something small, apply multiplication, and it grows. If God is doing the multiplying, there's no limit as to how large it can become. Pastor Phil Derstine found that out.

After teaching his congregation in Bradenton, Florida, about Jesus' parable of the talents (Matthew 25:14–30), Pastor Phil passed the offering plate. But instead of collecting money, he gave it away. Phil put a five dollar bill into each of 250 envelopes ($1200 in all) and instructed members of the church to "take and multiply" the money. Folks had thirty days. The only restriction was that they couldn't just return the five dollars unused. Like the servants in the parable, they had to risk what they'd been given in an effort to multiply it.

Ida Stump used her five dollars to buy ingredients for her favorite pizza. She hosted a pizza luncheon at her home. She took in about $100 in donations.

Jan Wright, crafty woman that she is, took her five dollars and bought supplies to make a little teddy-bear air freshener, which she sold for ten dollars. She used the ten dollars to buy supplies for two more and sold them. So she bought supplies for four and sold those. In the allotted month, she sold fifty versions of her creation, netting $495 in profit.

Nathan Weaver couldn't cook or sew, but as a teenager in the youth group he did know how to have fun. He used his five dollars to buy gas for the family boat. Then he rented out his boating services and for five dollars per person took people water skiing or for a ride.

One woman took her five dollars and bought material to make scarves, bringing in $310 in sales. A group of men pooled their money and sponsored a golf tournament. Other members pulled in a few bucks via bake sales. At the end of the thirty days, people brought back their multiplied monies. When it was tallied, that $1200 had mushroomed into $10,000—more than eight times the original amount.

"More rewarding than the financial return was to see everyone's hands on the oars," Phil said. "I simply challenged them to take the principles of God's Word they heard on Sunday and apply them to the plans of Monday."

God doesn't limit His multiplication efforts to money. He gives us joy in our personal lives. When we share that with others, He multiplies it in us and them beyond what we could ever imagine.

Try this experiment for the next thirty days: Make an effort to spread a little joy to your children each day, then keep a journal of how your efforts multiply in family members' lives. The results may surprise you.

Lord Jesus, multiply my efforts this month
as I attempt to spread joy into
the hearts of my children.

GRANDFATHER'S TABLE

Days of rest are down the road.
Days of delight are now before us.
—Bill Butterworth[53]

By the grace God has given me, I laid a foundation as an
expert builder, and someone else is building on it. But
each one should be careful how he builds.
1 Corinthians 3:10

Most of us cherish memories of sitting on a parent's lap and hearing a favorite story or settling into our cozy bed and listening to a story before fading away into sleep.

One favorite is from the Brothers Grimm. "The Old Grandfather's Table" involves a frail old man who went to live with his son, daughter-in-law, and four-year-old grandson. The old man's hands trembled, his eyesight was blurred, and his step faltered.

The family ate together at the table. But the elderly

grandfather's shaky hands and failing sight made eating difficult. Peas rolled off his spoon onto the floor. When he grasped the glass, milk spilled on the tablecloth. The son and daughter-in-law became irritated with the mess.

"We must do something about Grandfather," said the son. "I've had enough of his spilled milk, noisy eating, and food on the floor."

So husband and wife set a small table in the corner. There Grandfather ate alone while the rest of the family enjoyed dinner. Since Grandfather had broken a dish or two, his food was served in a wooden bowl. When the family glanced in Grandfather's direction, he sometimes had a tear in his eye as he sat alone. Still, the only words the couple had for him were sharp admonitions when he dropped a fork or spilled food.

The four-year-old grandson watched it all in silence.

One evening before supper, the father noticed his son playing with wood scraps on the floor. He asked the child sweetly, "What are you making?"

Just as sweetly the boy responded, "Oh, I'm making a little bowl for papa and mama to eat their food in when I grow up." The four-year-old smiled and went back to work. The words so struck the parents that they were speechless. Then tears started to stream down their cheeks. Though no words were spoken, both knew what must be done.

That evening the husband took Grandfather's hand

and gently led him back to the family table. For the remainder of his days he ate every meal with the family. And for some reason, neither husband nor wife seemed to care any longer when a fork was dropped, milk spilled, or the tablecloth soiled.

Children are remarkably perceptive. Their eyes ever observe, their ears ever listen, and their minds ever process the messages they absorb. If they see us patiently provide a happy home atmosphere for our family members, they will imitate that attitude for the rest of their lives. The wise parent realizes that every day the building blocks are being laid for the child's future. Let's be wise builders.

Dear Father, guide my thoughts
and actions today so my children
will see Your love, kindness,
and happiness in me.

A MOST UNUSUAL EXAM

So live that you wouldn't be ashamed to sell
the family parrot to the town gossip.
—Michael Hodgin[54]

A student is not above his teacher, but everyone who is
fully trained will be like his teacher.
Luke 6:40

The story is told of a young man with a passion for Jesus
and a desire to devote his life to service. The young
man applied to a mission board and was scheduled for an
interview to see if he was fit to send overseas to tell others
about Christ.

The appointment was set for 3 A.M., but the interviewer didn't arrive until 8 A.M. He introduced himself to
the applicant without apology for his late arrival.

"I have important questions to ask," he said. First, the
applicant was asked to spell the word baker. "B-A-K-E-R,"

221

he replied. Then he was asked the sum of 2 + 2. "Four," the candidate answered.

The interviewer stood, shook the candidate's hand, and said, "Well done. I will recommend your appointment to the mission board." The candidate left the room with a puzzled expression. It was the strangest interview he had ever experienced.

The examiner gave a glowing report of his interview with the candidate to the board: "He is well suited for missionary service."

One board member spoke up. "I'd like to know how you arrived at your decision." Others murmured, "Yes, I'd like to know, too."

"My first test involved self-denial. I asked the applicant to come at a time that would be very inconvenient and cost him sleep. He came without complaint. I wanted to know if he could be punctual. He arrived on time.

"I tested his patience. He had to wait five hours for me to appear. Would he be angry at my extended delay? He held his temper. Lastly I wanted to see his humility. I quizzed him with questions suited for a child. He answered politely and without offense.

"Men and women of the board, I am convinced our applicant will serve with devotion, humility, and integrity. I recommend that you appoint him at once." And they did.

We can't verify whether this incident occurred, but

in similar ways our character is tested (often imperceptibly) by our children:

"Daddy, tie my shoelace." (Will he act annoyed or do it cheerfully?)

In the midst of an important task: "Daddy, I need a drink of water. Will you get it now?"

"Daddy, why. . . ? But why. . . ? But Daddy, WHY. . . ?"

With such exams children measure the character of our life. When we respond with humility and grace, we become teachers of joy. We are missionary candidates. Our kids are the interviewers. When you arrive at your appointment today, will you ably answer your interviewer's questions? With God's help, you can.

Dear Jesus, teach me to
respond to life with joy so that I
may teach my children the same thing.

HE LOST THE WAR,
BUT WON THE HEARTS

The quality of a person's life is in direct proportion
to their commitment to excellence,
regardless of their chosen field of endeavor.
—Vince Lombardi

Therefore, as God's chosen people,
holy and dearly loved, clothe yourselves with
compassion, humility, gentleness, and patience.
Colossians 3:12

Our friend Dick has been greatly inspired by reading about General Robert E. Lee. He slipped a Lee biography to Norm and said, "This tells about a man who left behind a far-reaching legacy."

Lee is popularly remembered for his military leadership, but his character and kindness overshadow the military exploits. Children, youth, and adults alike were all attracted to him. Historian A. L. Long has found that people were continually touched by the general.[55] Once, for example, Lee was presiding over commencement at Washington College. A small lad wandered onto the platform, settled down at his feet, and rested his head on the president's knees. Lee suffered inconvenience rather than disturb the slumbering child.

On circus days the college president would escort a multitude of children. "He sat in the midst of them upon the boards of the tent, and it would have been difficult to estimate the relative amounts of enjoyment derived by him and his little guests," Long wrote.

Lee's letters to his own children blend humor, affection, and exhortation to godliness. To his eldest son Lee writes, "Say just what you mean to do on every occasion, and take it for granted you mean to do right. If a friend asks a favor, you should grant it, if it is reasonable; if not, tell him plainly why you cannot; you will wrong him and wrong yourself by equivocation of any kind."

Later he says, "Deal kindly but firmly with all your classmates; you will find it the policy which wears best. Above all, do not appear to others what you are not." Such counsel had deep and lasting power because it reflected the man's own integrity, love, and zest for life. They saw the same kindness and purity of heart that others saw.

Jefferson Davis, the president of the Confederacy,

said of Lee at his death, "I never in my life saw in him the slightest tendency to self-seeking. It was not his to make a record, it was not his to shift blame to others shoulders; but it was his, with an eye fixed upon the welfare of his country, never faltering, to follow the line of duty to the end."

Deuteronomy challenges fathers to incarnate a love and purity for the living God—heart, soul, and spirit. It was to be a vital reality, "so that you, your children and their children after them may fear the Lord your God as long as you live by keeping all his decrees and commands that I give you, and so that you may enjoy long life" (Deuteronomy 6:2).

We, too, receive this challenge to incarnate a vibrant life of faith and integrity, with its promised reward to enjoy long life. This is a heritage of indescribable value for children.

Dear God, help me to live my life
in such a way that my children
remember me as Robert E. Lee is remembered.

WHAT'S INSIDE COUNTS

*Character is the fundamental attribute of all
great leaders. It's more important than anything else.*
—General H. Norman Schwartzkopf

*If any man builds on this foundation using gold, silver,
costly stones, wood, hay or straw, his work will be shown
for what it is, because the Day will bring it to light.*
1 Corinthians 3:12–13

Mary is the kind of student who makes teaching fun. In a seminary class Norm teaches, one assignment asked students to submit a story they would use in a Bible teaching setting. Mary turned in a touching reflection of an experience with her father:

"I was visiting my parents. My father was eighty-six years old at the time. He's always worked circles around those much younger; he never had the sense that he was growing older. We were walking around the yard of his lovely California ranch home. My parents kept the house and yard in impeccable condition.

"Dad remarked, 'You know, Mary, I'm going to have to get a new roof on the house. Every time the wind blows some of the shingles work loose. Then I have to go up on the ladder and nail them down. I checked into a new shingle roof and was shocked to find out they will only guarantee it for twenty years. I've decided to get a slate roof. A slate roof will last a lifetime!' "

Mary's dad wants to outlive his lifetime. His character will outlast his earthly life because he will be known as a man who did what was best, not what was expedient or cheap. As his house endures, so will his memory.

Mary's memories may be similar to Serena's. Following her father's death, Serena and her sisters were going through his effects. She discovered an old pocket watch: "As I traced a finger on its tarnished case, I thought of how much the watch was like Dad. Plain, simple, and dependable."

Serena decided to give the watch to her son as a way to remember his grandfather. He went to have it cleaned and repaired. When the watch was returned, the jeweler made an interesting observation. He said that most pocket watches had expensive cases but inferior inner workings. In contrast, this case was simple and unadorned, but the inner workings were exceptional. The jeweler asked, "What sort of man would choose a watch like this?"

"He was like his watch," Serena says. "Modest on the outside, but inside pure gold."[56]

Inner beauty in their fathers has filled Mary and Serena with a joyful admiration for these men in their lives. Their children will inevitably benefit from this admiration, too. The beauty of inner character is a constant source of joy, and always seems to endure like pure gold.

Dear Lord, we know that others watch our lives.
Empower us that they may see the
beauty of Jesus Christ in us.

THAT'S A PROMISE

*I've learned that kind words and good deeds are eternal.
You never know where their influence will end.*
—a fifty-one-year-old

*If you belong to Christ, then you are Abraham's seed,
and heirs according to the promise.*
Galatians 3:29

Joey Rao's grandpa sat at the kitchen table using salt and pepper shakers to illustrate the solar eclipse that would occur that afternoon. He couldn't begin to realize how the conversation would lead to an adventure that would influence young Joey's future.

Joey and his grandpa watched the "mysterious sky show" that afternoon. His grandfather told him that they had seen only a partial eclipse. "We should have gone to Maine," Grandpa said. "There the eclipse was total."

Grandpa didn't let the matter drop. He investigated

and discovered the next total eclipse would occur in Florida, seven years later, in March.

"Make a note on the calendar," he said to little Joe. "We're going. That's a promise."

In the intervening years, Joe's parents divorced, so Joe, his mother, and sister moved in with his grandparents. The grandfather became an important influence in the boy's life. Grandpa nurtured a love for astronomy, taking him to the Hayden Planetarium, eventually buying him a telescope. They spent many evenings in the backyard gazing skyward.

Then Joe's granddad developed hoarseness; it was cancer. His voice box had to be removed—the day before the Florida eclipse. The trip to Florida could not occur, but Grandfather remembered how important a promise was. When Joe visited his grandpa in the hospital, the man scrawled on a piece of paper:

"Did you watch the eclipse?"

Joe nodded.

"When's the next one?"

Joe knew the answer: It would be a couple years later over the Canadian Maritimes.

His grandfather wrote, "We'll be there," and smiled.

Grandpa learned to speak by gulping air, and he and Joe returned to their love for stargazing and waited for the next eclipse. As the event drew near, they made plans for the 900-mile trip. They would travel in a well-worn Plymouth Fury with Grandmother, Mom, and Sister joining the grand adventure.

When the family arrived in the tiny town of Cap-Chat, Quebec, clouds threatened to hide the eclipse. The family found a grassy spot and set up the telescope. Then the wait. The clouds held back and the wonder of a full solar eclipse took place.

"I would never forget that miraculous day—or the man of blunted dreams who had awakened in me a deep awe of the universe and a sense of my own possibilities."

Joe Rao is now an instructor at the Hayden Planetarium and plans to take his children to the Caribbean to watch a total solar eclipse. He tells them, "Make a note on the calendar. We're all going. That's a promise."[57]

Lord Jesus, enable my children—
and grandchildren—
to experience the joy of my promise kept.

A LITTLE VISION GOES
A LONG, LONG WAY

*The composer Igor Stravinsky once wrote a
new piece that contained a difficult violin passage.
After several weeks of rehearsal, the solo violinist came
to Stravinsky and said that he could not play it.
He had given it his best effort but found
the passage too difficult, even unplayable.
Stravinsky replied, "I understand that. What I am after
is the sound of someone trying to play it."*
—Philip Yancey (*Church: Why Bother?*[58])

*By faith Isaac blessed Jacob and
Esau in regard to their future.*
Hebrews 11:20

Pat McGee could taste the victory, could see it, smell it,
practically touch it. A senior at St. Peter's High
School, he was in a friendly game between the senior and

the sophomore basketball teams. And he set his sights on nothing less than a victory.

Those sophomores played tough, error-free basketball. The score remained close. Then one of the seniors fouled out of the game. Then another. And another. With four minutes left in the game, the scored was tied at 32— and all the seniors on the team had fouled out except Pat.

Pat determined to win the game by himself. So, for the final four minutes, it was five players against Pat. Passing, dribbling, shooting, pressure all the time.

When the clock finally ticked its last second, the final score was 35 to 32—in favor of the seniors. Not only had Pat kept all five opposing players from scoring, he had made three points himself and single-handedly won the game.[59]

Pat probably should have given up. But he kept his eyes on the goal, and he achieved success beyond his wildest dreams. Others have done that:

❖ NBA legend Michael Jordan was cut from his high school basketball team. He kept working and made the team the next year, then went on to become a superstar.

❖ After his English ship was torpedoed during World War II, Poon Lim escaped on a life raft on November 23, 1942. He was rescued April 5, 1943—four and one-half months later.

- ❖ Al had difficulty with simple math equations, and his wife helped him fill out his tax returns. But Albert Einstein didn't let that learning disability stop him from creating the complex theories that led to the development of nuclear energy.

- ❖ In 1944 the director of the Blue Book Modeling Agency turned away young Norma Jean Baker, who hoped to be a model, telling her, "You'd better learn secretarial work or else get married." Norma became better known as Marilyn Monroe.

- ❖ In 1954 the manager of the Grand Ole Opry fired an up-and-coming singer after one performance, advising him to go back to driving a truck. But the singer, named Elvis Presley, pursued music as a career anyway.

- ❖ Thomas Edison failed in more than 2000 attempts to invent a practical lightbulb.

- ❖ British fighter pilot Douglas Bader lost both his legs in a crash but continued to fly in World War II. He was captured three times—and escaped each time in spite of his disability.

- ❖ General Douglas MacArthur enrolled in West Point Military Academy after being rejected twice.

❖ Louis L'Amour's novels have sold more than 200 million copies, but his first book was rejected 350 times by publishers.

In the face of temporary setbacks and distractions, all of these people were able to maintain a clear vision of what they wanted. You, too, will fail sometimes as you work toward creating a legacy of joy for your children. But like Pat McGee, Michael Jordan, Poon Lim, and the others, you can succeed beyond your wildest dreams if you never lose sight of your vision. Remember, when it comes to leaving a legacy for your children, a little vision goes a long, long way.

Jesus, give me clarity of vision
for the future of my kids
and the power to overcome
obstacles that may interfere.

HALL HOCKEY AND OTHER DIVERSIONS

In every child there's a hero.
—BeBe and CeCe Winans, "We Can Make a Difference"

*Give, and it will be given
to you. A good measure, pressed down, shaken together
and running over, will be poured into your lap.*
Luke 6:38

"During my years of fatherhood," says Mike, "my son, Tony, and I have invented all sorts of wacky games to play around the house. Our sole purpose in these games is to have fun (and not break things).

"We've got some great games: Hall Hockey; Quarterback Attack (in which a football is thrown through holes in a piece of holey cardboard); Bean Bag Baseball; Nerf War; Living Room Soccer; and Elvis Olympics (shaking up to the tune of 'All Shook Up').

"Our favorites are the Bed Games: Catch-a-Pass-While-Diving-onto-the-Bed; King of the Bed; Quick-Toss/Big-Toss/Flip-Toss onto the Bed; Trampoline Practice; and Pro Wrestling Parody.

"We've seen our share of broken lamps, torn fabric, messy covers, carpet burns. Once a coffee table split in half. But it's been worth it all to hear Tony's delighted laughter with each new rule we've made up over the years.

"Just after Tony's seventh birthday, I was diagnosed with a chronic stomach illness that leaves me battling nausea on a daily basis. Needless to say, that's hampered my ability to fully engage in our evening entertainment. In fact, I'm often left as a cheering spectator for Quarterback Attack or Living Room Soccer.

"As I write this book, my wife, Amy, and I are in the process of adopting a little brother or sister for Tony. One evening, Tony and I were chatting about what it will be like to have this happy addition to our family. I'll admit I was feeling a bit melancholy.

" 'Tony,' I said, 'your little brother or sister will never know what I was like before I got sick. That child won't get to play all our fun games, at least not as much as you and I did. I just can't do it anymore.' I sighed. 'That makes me feel sad.'

"Then Tony cocked his head, grinned, and looked me squarely in the eyes. 'Dad,' he said, 'you're forgetting something.'

" 'What?' I said dolefully.

" 'Our new baby will have something I didn't have: me! When the baby's big enough, I'll play Hall Hockey with it. I'll teach a little brother or sister how to play Bed Games. I'll show him or her how to play all the games we've played. So even if you can't always play with the new baby, I still can. And I will.'

"I realized then that my son is not only inheriting a legacy of joy; he's already beginning to pass it on to others as well. And that makes this father's heart smile."

Dear Lord, strengthen me to sow seeds of joy
in my children's lives today and every day. Amen!

NOTES

1. Anecdotes from Ross and Kathryn Petras, *The 176 Stupidest Things Ever Done* (New York: Main Street Books, 1996).
2. Quotation and statistics from David Blankenhorn, *Fatherless America* (New York: HarperPerennial, n.d.). Other statistics from Ken Canfield, *The Heart of a Father* (Chicago: Northfield, 1996); George Barna, *Generation Next* (Ventura, Calif.: Regal); and James Patterson and Peter Kim, *The Day America Told the Truth* (New York: Prentice Hall).
3. Nashville: Thomas Nelson, 1997.
4. Paul C. Brownlow, ed (Fort Worth: Brownlow, 1997), 64.
5. 16 January 1962.
6. Quotations from syndicated Cal Thomas column, "Fathers: Much to Learn," 17 June 1990.
7. "'Oasis' Gallagher Angry at Dad." *Loveland Reporter-Herald.* August 17, 1997.
8. H. B. London, Jr., and Stan Toler (Tulsa: Honor, 1997), 67.
9. New York: Avon, 1975.
10. Quotation and story from William Burks, Jr., "Like Father, Like Son," *Guideposts,* August 1996.
11. James A. Hefley, *Dictionary of Illustrations* (Grand Rapids: Zondervan, 1971).
12. Michael Hodgin, comp. (Grand Rapids: Zondervan, 1994).
13. Sue Schumann, "A Shot in the Arm," *Christian Single,* March 1997, 28–31.
14. Dandi Daley Mackall (Tulsa: Trade Life, 1997), 14.
15. New York: Delacorte, 1993.
16. *Loony Laws* (New York: Walker and Company), 1990.
17. Grand Rapids: Zondervan, 1997.
18. Grand Rapids: HarperCollins, 1997.
19. "Are Dads Really Tuned In to Their Children?" *Today's Father.* Volume 4, Number 2, 1996.
20. "Fathers in America." National Center for Fathering press kit materials.
21. Tim Burke and Christine Burke, *Major League Dad* (Colorado Springs: Focus on the Family, 1994).
22. Grand Rapids: Zondervan, 1995.
23. Virginia Hearn, ed., *What They Did Right* (Wheaton, Ill.: Tyndale, 1974).
24. *What They Did Right.*
25. David Heller, *Dear God* (New York: Doubleday, 1987), 75.
26. *Kids Say the Cutest Things About Dads.*
27. New York: Dell, 1990.
28. *My Kids Are My Best Teachers* (Old Tappan, N.J.: Revell, 1986).
29. *The 176 Stupidest Things Ever Done.*
30. Ibid.
31. Dallas: Word.
32. Quoted in *God's Little Devotional Book II* (Tulsa: Honor, 1997), 66.
33. H. Jackson Brown, Jr., *Live, Learn, and Pass It On* (Nashville: Rutledge Hill, 1991).
34. Quoted in "The Opportunity of Fatherhood," National Center for Fathering press kit.
35. Quoted in *God's Little Devotion Book for Dads* (Tulsa: Honor, 1995).
36. Quoted in H. Jackson Brown, Jr., *A Father's Book of Wisdom* (Nashville: Rutledge Hill, 1988), 18.
37. Tulsa: Honor, 1997.
38. Grand Rapids: Baker, 1996.
39. H. B. London, Jr., and Stan Toler (Tulsa: Honor, 1997), 109.
40. Ron Mehl, *Meeting God at a Dead End* (Sisters, Ore.: Multnomah, 1996).
41. *Letters Home* (Nashville: Cumberland House, 1997).
42. Paul C. Brownlow, ed. (Fort Worth: Brownlow, 1997).
43. Grand Rapids: Zondervan, 1995.
44. New York: John Wiley & Sons, 1994.
45. "The Opportunity of Fatherhood."
46. "A Father's Legacy," *Men of Action,* Summer 1996, 4–5.
47. "Get-a Grip" *People Magazine,* March 23, 1998.
48. Gerald Harris, *Olympic Heroes* (Nashville: Broadman & Holman, 1996).
49. Quoted in John Drescher, *Seven Things Children Need* (Scottdale, Pa.: Herald, 1976).
50. Becky Beane, "Celebrating Our 15th Season" *The Angel Tree Herald* 2.3 (Fall 1996), 2.
51. *1001 Humorous Illustrations.*
52. Helen Hosier, comp., *The Quotable Christian* (Uhrichsville, Ohio: Barbour, 1998).
53. *My Kids Are My Best Teachers.*
54. *1001 Humorous Illustrations.*
55. *Memoirs of Robert E. Lee* (Secaucus, N.J.: Blue and Gray, 1983).
56. Serena Miller, "Inner Workings," *Guideposts,* September 1997.
57. Joe Rao, "The Promise," *Reader's Digest,* November 1997, 10–13.
58. Grand Rapids: Zondervan, 1998, 99.
59. *The Boy Who Sold 10 Million Crickets* (New York: Parachute, 1991), 12.